The Cherry Blossom Festival
Sakura Celebration

ANN McCLELLAN

BUNKER HILL PUBLISHING
BOSTON

in association with
The National Cherry Blossom Festival®

To the Japanese Cherry Trees,
whose ethereal and evanescent blooming
lifts our spirits and makes us all poets.

NATIONAL
Cherry
Blossom ®
F·E·S·T·I·V·A·L

www.bunkerhillpublishing.com

First published in 2005 by Bunker Hill Publishing Inc.
26 Adams Street, Charlestown, MA 02129 USA

10 9 8 7 6 5 4 3 2 1

Library of Congress Cataloging in Publication Data available from the publisher's office

ISBN 1 59373 040 3

Designed by Louise Millar
Copyedited by George T. Kosar, Ph.D., The Sarov Press.

Printed in China

Contents

Ducks make better neighbors than beavers for the Japanese cherry trees around the Tidal Basin. In 1999, several of the trees were felled and others damaged by industrious beavers, tempted by the trees' proximity to the water's edge.

Introduction

Crowds from all social classes, including visitors from the west with their pet dog enjoy cherry blossom viewing. Utagawa Hiroshige (1842?-1894), Cherry Blossoms in Full Bloom along Sumida River, *from* The Most Beautiful Place in Tokyo, *Woodblock print triptych.*

The trees forming the cloud of pink blossoms around the Tidal Basin each spring are now as well known around the world as other landmarks of the Nation's Capital such as the U.S. Capitol Building and the White House. It wasn't always so, and how they came to Washington and what they mean to the city and the nation today is a fascinating story.

The National Cherry Blossom Festival® serves as an umbrella organization to coordinate the activities, events, and educational programs held to honor the flowering cherry trees and the friendship between Japan and America. Celebrating the arrival of spring in Washington, D.C., Festival participants come from throughout the Metropolitan Washington area, across the country, and from many nations, especially Japan.

The Cherry Blossom Festival, Sakura Celebration captures the history and significance of the trees in Japan, the perseverance of those who envisioned them lining Washington's water banks and roadways, and the range of uplifting, multi-faceted events of today's Festival.

The National Cherry Blossom Festival® is pleased to be associated with this comprehensive overview of the Festival and its origins, and hopes that it will enhance your enjoyment and appreciation of all that it encompasses each spring.

G. Bradley Elmore, President,
2005 National Cherry Blossom Festival Board of Directors

Japanese Cherry Trees
Their Roots and Traditions

Painted after Edo (Tokyo) was rebuilt following a destructive fire in 1657, this 17th-century screen shows city dwellers flocking to Ueno Park to enjoy cherry blossom viewing. Hishikawa Moronobu (1615–1694) Viewing Cherry Blossoms at Ueno Park, *Ink, color and gold on paper, 165.6 H x 367.8 W cm.*

Cherry Blossoms in Ancient Japan

Oh my . . . Oh my . . .
Was all I could say
Of the flowers on Mount Yoshino

Yasubara Teishitsu (1609-73)

Aged cherry trees bloom along a riverbank near Edo, modern Tokyo, with Mount Fuji in the distance. Everyday life continues underneath the beautiful blossoms, and a group on a platform under the trees drinks tea or sake. Utagawa Hiroshige, (1797–1858), Sunset at Koganei Bridge, *Woodblock print*

The breathtaking sight of the cherry trees blooming in Japan has inspired princes, poets, artists, and ordinary people for over 1000 years. The ornamental cherry trees' blossoms, called sakura, are as closely associated with the image of Japan held by the rest of the world as is Mount Fuji.

Like Mount Fuji, the cherry blossoms have a spiritual meaning for the Japanese people. The sublime beauty of the flowers and their brief life at the beginning of each spring symbolize the essence of a human's short life well-lived. As the poet Motoöri famously expressed it: "If one should ask you concerning the spirit of a true Japanese, point to the wild cherry blossom glowing in the sun."

One of the legends suggesting why the cherry trees' blossoms are so exquisite and ephemeral says that the fairy Ko-no-hana-sakuya-hime, the "maiden who causes trees to bloom," hovers low in the spring sky, awakening the sleeping trees with her delicate breath. This magical quality of the blossoms is expressed in art and literature, even in music. The traditional Japanese folk song, "Sakura, sakura," for example, celebrates the flowers in the following way:

> *Cherry Blossoms, cherry blossoms.*
> *Across March skies*
> *As far as you can see.*
> *Mists or clouds?*
> *Their fragrance is floating.*
> *Let us go, let us go*
>   *It's a must to see!*

The remarkable qualities of the cherry blossom trees' blooming inspired blossom viewing rituals and traditions that the Japanese emperors and their court

The cloud-like effect of the wild cherry trees in bloom on Mount Yoshino has inspired poets and common folk in Japan for over a thousand years, and plantings of the trees aspire to emulate the ethereal quality found in nature. Katsushika Hokusai (1760–1849), Cherry Flowers at Yoshino, *1836, Woodblock print.*

had established by the 9th century, C.E. Called *hanami*, cherry blossom viewing practices and patterns evolved over time from the early court traditions, expanding to include the samurai during the period of their rule under the Shogunate, and later adopted by common people as well.

Today, when the cherry trees bloom Japanese people from all walks of life and throughout the archipelago participate in *hanami* and further celebrate the return of spring with a festival called a *Sakura Matsuri. Matsuri,* Japanese folk festivals with roots in Shinto religious observances, are held throughout the year for many different occasions. Now their role is more profane than religious, with an emphasis on entertainment, although they help keep ancient traditions alive and serve as community-building activities.

Samurai Spirit

The brief and exuberant blooming of the Japanese cherry trees was an important symbol for the samurai warriors. Their highly disciplined life as cultured men of war had as a highest goal to die an honorable death, preferably in the service of their overlord and in the prime of life. This same feeling compelled the kamikaze pilots to perform their astonishing feats during World War II, ensuring their certain death at a young age in service to their country. To the samurai, the blooming of the cherry trees signified the beauty of a brief life well-lived, its petals falling from the tree in their prime.

The Way of the Warrior, or *Bushido*, evolved in Japan during the Heian period (794–1195) when warriors such as Yosiie and Yoshitsune lived, performing their audacious military tactics and demonstrating mythic personal bravery and self-discipline. Beyond their highly developed skills in warfare, samurai warriors cultivated a refined private life, adhering to a code of honor respectful of their ancestors, and also the aged and the weak. They valued skillful practice of many arts, now considered essential Japanese traditions, such as ikebana flower arranging, calligraphy, poetry writing, Noh dramas, and the tea ceremony.

Samurai ruled Japan under shoguns from the 12th century to the mid-19th century when their potency was eclipsed by the Meiji Restoration, which centralized power again under the Emperor, and propelled Japan into the modern era after its opening by Commodore Matthew C. Perry in 1854.

Cherry blossoms fall as the great warrior Minamoto no Yoshiie makes his way south following successful military campaigns in the barbarian region beyond the Nakoso Barrier. Yoshiie's exploits inspired many myths from the Heian Period (794-1185). He wrote the poem inscribed in the upper portion of the painting:

> Although I thought/that the blowing wind would not come
> to the Barrier of Nakoso
> the mountain cherries fall so/that they make the path very narrow.

Sumiyoshi Hironao (1781-1828) and Yokoyama Ikei (ca. 1818–1829), Minamoto no Yoshiie at Nakoso Barrier, *Hanging Scroll, Ink, color and gold on silk.*

Members of the first official Japanese delegation sent to the United States in 1860, possibly its three doctors, were photographed in Matthew Brady's studio in Washington, DC. Their shaved heads and paired swords and daggers indicate their rank as samurai.

Considered one of the greatest samurai, Minamoto no Yoshitsune (1159–1189) is shown with his loyal band of warriors under a blooming cherry tree. The exploits of Yoshitsune and his brother Yoritomo, later the first shogun, and their successful defeat of the Taira clan form the basis of the Tales of the Heike, *like the* Iliad *in the scope of its expression in many Japanese art forms. The story of Yoshitsune's legendary courage and prowess, culminating in his betrayal and early death by suicide, has inspired many Japanese myths and dramas. Ishikawa Komei, Carved elephant tusk vase, ca. 1880.*

The spirit of the samurai still exists in Japan today. Famous battles are re-enacted, complete with armor, though without the traditional razor-edged swords, and martial arts are widely practiced, ensuring continued familiarity with *Bushido*. The elements of *Bushido* emphasized in Japan today are about overcoming one's self-defeating perceptions and assumptions, trying to do one's best, and living life honorably and to the full.

11

Privacy and separation from each other and from the common people were important to the members of the Japanese Imperial Court and the nobles. Aristocratic ladies were specially protected from view by curtains, folding screens, and bamboo blinds.

Folding screens were used to delineate and set the tone of interior spaces of Japanese palaces and dwellings. They also were set up to create defined spaces out of doors where they provided protection from prying eyes and masked unattractive views. A beautiful screen placed anywhere enhanced its environs, inside or out, and served as an object of contemplation.

The privacy created by the screens or drapes hung under the blooming cherry trees in the spring or under the flame-colored foliage of the Japanese maple trees in the fall allowed for a number of activities. Picnics were common, and the food was transported in layered boxes called *jubako* with separate compartments for different foods such as rice, fish, vegetables, and pickles.

Poetry was composed and written in calligraphic style, using a portable writing box or *suzuri-bako*. These boxes contained a sloping ink-stone, the *suzuri*, which was rubbed with an ink-stick and mixed with water to produce ink.

Musical instruments such as the *shamisen* (similar to a three-stringed lute), a bamboo flute, or a *koto* (like a large zither) were played for the listening pleasure of the *hanami* participants or to inspire dancers, as they still do today.

Inros are small, sectioned containers originally used to hold official seals and inkpads. About two or three inches long, they hung by a cord from waist sashes, secured by netsukes or carved toggles. Inro later were used to carry medicines or cosmetics, and now are prized collectibles because of their artful and high quality workmanship. Shunsui, Edo Period (1603–1868), Inro, lacquer with black ground.

A 17th-century Japanese screen illustrates the thirty-fourth chapter in the Tales of Genji, *one of the world's oldest novels. An escaping cat causes a bamboo screen to lift, revealing the secluded Third Princess to nobles playing kemari, a courtly form of kickball, under blooming cherry trees, leading ultimately to her seduction by one of them. Tosa Mitsuoki (1617–1691),* The Visit of Sochi and Kashiwagi to the New Palace, *from the* Tales of Genji, *Detail of Screen, Ink, color and gold on paper.*

"Rooms" under the blooming trees were created by using folding screens, hanging bolts of cloth between vertical poles, or suspending ropes between the trees for curtains, as shown here. The unpredictable weather typical of the cherry blossom-viewing season in Japan is reflected in the windblown drapery. Wind-screen and cherry tree, Screen, *Edo period (1615–1868), Color over gold on paper.*

Cherry Blossoms in Japanese Poetry

Japanese oral traditions evolved quickly into written literature once the Chinese writing system was adopted in Japan in the 8th century, C.E. By the middle of that century, the *Manyoshu*, the oldest anthology of Japanese poetry, was compiled, and in the 11th century, Lady Murasaki Shikibu wrote the *Tale of Genji*.

Japanese poems are short and typically address experiences from daily life, love and nature. The oldest and longest type of poem is called tanka. It has thirty-one syllables in five lines in a sequence of 5-7-5-7-7 syllables. Haiku, the shorter type of poem, has seventeen syllables in three lines in a sequence of 5-7-5 syllables.

The evanescent beauty of the cherry blossoms has inspired Japanese poets for more than a thousand years. Here are two examples:

> *This gathered cherry branch can scarce convey*
> *A fancy of the blossom-laden tree:*
> *Blooming in sunlight, could I view it there*
> *Thoughts of its beauty would drive sleep away.*
>
> Emperor Shomu to his lady love, 8th century

> *Even if the cherry flowers bloom*
> *Ours is a world of suffering.*
>
> Issa (1763–1827)

Pictured at a 19th-century cherry blossom-viewing party in Tokyo's Ueno Park, a young boy ties a poem to a cherry tree's bloom-laden branch, repeating a Japanese tradition with roots in the 8th century when Japan developed its own writing system based on the Chinese. Toyohara Chikanobu (1838–1912), Snow, Moon, Flower-Edo; Flower of Ueno, Cherry Blossoms at Mt. Toei, *Ink on paper, 325.44 x 215.9mm.*

Works by different poets collected in a medieval Japanese poetry anthology were painted as if on tanzaku or slips of paper on this screen commissioned about 1675 by the Empress Tofukumon. It suggests the bitter-sweet time following a blossom-viewing party, when the poems inspired by the beauty of nature are left to blow away in the wind. Tosa Mitsuoki (1617-1691), Flowering Cherry with Poem Slips, c. 1675. One of a pair of six-fold screens, Ink, colors and gold on silk, c. 1675, 142.5 x 293.2 cm.

Two geishas read while falling cherry blossoms remind them that life is fleeting. Perhaps they are reading the Tale of Genji, considered by many the world's oldest novel, written about the year 1000 and including nearly eight hundred poems. Gakutei Harunobu, 19th century, Two Geishas Reading from a Book, Hanging scroll, Color, gold and silver on silk, 56.6 x 87.0 cm.

15

Cherry Blossom Viewing Traditions in Japan

Mount Goten on the outskirts of Tokyo, overlooking Tokyo Bay, has been a favorite destination for Japanese hanami *or cherry blossom viewing for centuries. Picnics under the trees often include sake drinking as well as dancing and music-making. Ando Hiroshige (1797-1858),* Famous Places of the Eastern Capital, *c. 1832-1855, Woodblock print 33.97 x 75.57 cm.*

Sake, wine made from fermented rice, has played an important role in Japanese culture since wet-rice cultivation was introduced to the archipelago from mainland Asia. Initially restricted to the Imperial Court and important temples and shrines, sake still is considered a special beverage by the Japanese, and is served at celebratory occasions and traditional ceremonies. Even today, brewers will offer a barrel from a fresh batch of sake to their local Shinto shrine as a gift to the god, or *kami,* and to ask for the god's blessing.

Sake can be drunk hot or cold, from glasses or ceramic or wooden cups. It is customary to wait until everyone is served, and their cups raised in a salute, calling out "kampai" before taking a drink of sake.

Japanese serve each other, filling their companions' empty glasses rather than their own.

Cherry blossom-viewing picnics traditionally included drinking sake, with portable kegs, warmers, cups and cup washers. Today, imbibing alcoholic beverages while participating in cherry blossom viewing or *hanami* continues to be typical in Japan.

As an anonymous haiku poem says:

Without flowing wine
How to enjoy lovely
Cherry Blossoms?

Japanese courtesans often are shown wearing their obis *tied in front around their many-layered robes, and their distinguishing hairstyles include long, decorative hair sticks. Courtesans were associated with cherry blossoms because of their shared ephemeral beauty. Hosoda Eishi (1756–1829),* Beauties of the Season - Spring, *early 19th century, Detail, Full color on silk, 175.6 x 49.8 cm.*

Japanese Woodblock Prints

The privacy drape rolled over her shoulders and a supply of sake in wrapped barrels show that this geisha is ready for hanami, *as indicated by the cherry blossoms drooping into the left-hand corner of a 19th-century woodblock print. Utagawa Toyokuni III, Woodblock print ca. 1847–52.*

Printing was used in Japan to reproduce images as early as the 8th century, C.E., though it only came into its own as an art form in the second half of the 17th century when the capital moved to Tokyo, then called Edo. Its growing and vibrant economy and urban culture were driven largely by merchants and craftsmen who demanded art reflecting their experiences and dreams, rather than the formal and refined imagery inspired by court rituals and tastes.

Many of the woodblock prints from the Edo period (1603–1868) are called *Ukiyo-e* or "pictures of the floating world." Rooted in the Buddhist view that human life is short-lived, it later came to have fashion-related and hedonistic overtones. *Ukiyo-e* prints first featured Kabuki actors and courtesans from the pleasure quarters, then later expanded into landscapes and locations across the country. The colors, patterns and perspectives used in *Ukiyo-e* prints inspired western artists such as Monet, Whistler and Cassatt.

Cherry blossoms are closely associated with women in Japanese art, especially with geishas and courtesans of Japan's pleasure quarters. The brief, transcendent beauty of the blossoms symbolized the transitory and enjoyable nature of visits to the pleasure quarters.

Yoshiwara in Tokyo and Shimabara in Kyoto were two famous pleasure quarters where men went for many different entertainments in addition to legalized prostitution. Dancing, music-making, poetry writing, singing, eating and drinking all were found in the pleasure quarters.

The first geishas were men who were professional entertainers in 17th-century Kyoto. Gradually, more women than men became geishas and men took on the role of jesters, setting off the women's refined presentation of the traditional performing arts. Both entertained the customers of the pleasure quarters and the clients of the courtesans.

A geisha's training is strenuous and she must pass an exam before she joins a *kemban* or geisha registry office. She continues to study the traditional arts throughout her professional career which can be life-long because it emphasizes her skills rather than her looks.

Courtesans with elaborate coiffures, front-tied padded kimonos and tall platform footwear called geta *parade under the cherry blossoms in Yoshiwara, a pleasure district in Tokyo, surrounded by many attendants including geishas and young girl attendants. Artist unknown,* Festival at Yoshiwara, *Ink on paper, 33.81 x 46.83 cm.*

Today, geishas provide entertainment at particular restaurants or teahouses where they sing, dance, or play Japanese musical instruments, especially the *shamisen* or three-stringed lute. Geishas are known also for being good conversationalists and amusing companions for social occasions.

Two women dance in private, protected from on-lookers by folding screens decorated with images of cherry blossoms and clouds. The joyful exuberance possible in the pleasure quarters is expressed in their dynamic movement. Utagawa Toyokuni III, 1852, Woodblock print, oban.

Musume Dojoji is a famous Kabuki play, adapted from an earlier Noh play. The story is about a maiden who, spurned in her love for a priest, is transformed by jealousy into a giant serpent or dragon. In Kabuki theater, all the roles are played by men. Utagawa Kunisada, (1786-1864), The Actor Bando Mitsugoro III as the Maiden of Dojoji, Woodblock print, 1816, 36.3 x 25.6 cm, oban.

19

Parades and Processions

Experiencing the beauty of the cherry blossoms in groups has been a pattern for *hanami* in Japan for centuries. After surviving another winter, grateful worshippers made their way to a shrine or temple to offer their thanks. The Emperor and his court paid official visits to shrines or cherry blossom-viewing locations in large, well-ordered processions.

Parades were also prominent features of *matsuri* or festivals, as they still are today. The original purpose of the festival was to bring the *kami* or god into the community and spread its divine power among the people and across the land. The processions evolved to invoke the *kami* and then accompany it on its journey from its home shrine to its temporary one for the festival. They also were intended to impress the *kami* with the participants' fervor and devotion.

Other memorable processions occurred when the samurai princes or *daimyo* moved their entire households between the capital and their own lands. The *daimyo* were required to live in Edo (now Tokyo) every other year to protect and serve the shogun. Their annual migrations had the intended side-effect of preventing them from consolidating power in their own domains, and they also impressed onlookers with the force available to the shogun, helping to maintain the shogunate's tight control in Japan.

The Taisho Emperor and Empress are shown leaving Yasukuni Shrine in Tokyo, a Shinto shrine dedicated to Japanese war dead. The Taisho Emperor (1879-1926) was the first emperor to be educated publicly. Under his rule imperial monogamy was established and for the first time his children were allowed to live with him. The statue in the upper left-hand corner is of Saigo Takamori, Japan's last samurai. Takamori helped overthrow the shogunate, then became disillusioned with the new government and fought it unsuccessfully in the Satsuma Rebellion of 1877. Artist unknown, Taisho Emperor and Empress.

An 18th-century scroll depicts famous places in Kyoto in each of the four seasons, showing the importance of both Buddhist temples and Shinto shrines to pilgrims. Cherry blossoms in clouds of white indicate the early spring season as a group of samurai and their ladies make their way among the sacred sites. *Kawashima Shigenobu (ca. 1722– 1744), Handscroll, Ink, color and gold on paper, 33.0 x 829.0 cm.*

Finely dressed women of the Imperial Court and their attendants are shown leaving Edo, modern Tokyo, heading west to view the cherry blossoms with Mount Fuji in the background. This scene mocks the elaborate processions that were mounted by the daimyo *on their way to and from the capital city to enhance the perception of their power. Ando Hiroshige II (1826–1869),* Flower Paths: Procession of Women, *1857, Woodblock print, 366.71 x 746.13mm.*

Japonism

Japonism is the name later historians have given the craze for all things Japanese that followed the opening of Japan by Commodore Matthew Perry in 1854. The London Exhibition of 1862 included a small Japanese Court, and the Paris Exposition in 1867 and the Philadelphia Centennial Exposition of 1876 had larger displays that tantalized visitors with exhibits from the mysterious and previously unknown archipelago. Tales told by whalers lucky to return from encounters with the Japanese no longer seemed so preposterous or unbelievable.

Just as they had "fallen" for Chinese art and objects in the heyday of the China trade in the 18th century, Europeans and Americans were enchanted by Japanese aesthetics and styles. The discovery of Japanese prints, their visual freedom, use of color and modes of composition changed how many artists in the West developed their own art, as seen in the works of Claude Monet, James McNeill Whistler, Mary Cassatt, Childe Hassam and William Merritt Chase, among others.

The rave for things Japanese extended beyond the fine arts to include furniture, textiles, porcelains, metalwork and plants, and Japanese suppliers were

Whistler's Caprice in Purple and Gold *exemplifies Japonism in every respect. From the European model—who was the artist's Irish mistress dressed in a luxurious kimono—to the Japanese prints by Hiroshige in her hand and arrayed before her on the floor, to the close-in perspective chosen by the artist, and including the Japanese screen appearing in the background, all these elements show how a western artist incorporated Japanese elements in his work. James McNeill Whistler (1834–1903),* Caprice in Purple and Gold: The Golden Screen, *1864, Oil on wood, 50.2 x 68.7 cm.*

eager to try to meet the demand. Industrial Exhibitions were held in Japan to encourage familiarity with Japanese goods and encourage trade. Cherry trees were among the "products" that were exported, first to Europe and later to the United States.

On an unofficial and occasional basis, some sailors would bring home seeds or saplings which grew under the right conditions. One such tree in northwest Washington, D.C., inspired a cherry blossom-viewing and tea ceremony party held in 1905, attended by Eliza Scidmore with David Fairchild and Marian Bell as an engaged couple among other guests. Only fifty years after Perry's landmark treaty opening the country, all in the group were well-versed in Japanese practices and traditions, and wanted to bring them to the fore to benefit America and her capital city.

The combination of high-quality craftsmanship and refined aesthetics made Japanese objects prized among artists and collectors in the West. The cherry blossoms and clouds remind the bearer of this inro of the beauty of the trees and the transitory nature of a life well-lived. Artist unknown, Edo Period 1603-1868, Inro, Lacquer, mother-of-pearl and gold-foil inlays.

The Japanese were eager to export their products as well as their aesthetics to the rest of the world and the Second Industrial Exhibition was held in 1881 in Tokyo's Ueno Park, famous for its cherry trees. Western influences also made their way to Japan as the ladies' bell-shaped skirts and boots and the Emperor in an Admiral's uniform show. Toyohara Kunichika (1835-1900), Tokyo Ueno Second Industrial Exhibition, 1881., Woodblock print, oban triptych, 35.7 x 71.8 cm

23

A Gift from Japan
A National Treasure in Washington

The Capitol Building is seen in the distance beyond the blooming cherry trees prior to 1920 in a glass slide from the archives of the Office of Public Buildings and Grounds.

A New Idea for Washington

Four people witnessed Mrs. Taft plant the first cherry tree around the Tidal Basin in 1912: the Ambassador from Japan and his wife, Viscountess Chinda, Colonel Spencer Cosby, then the Superintendent of Public Buildings and Grounds, and Miss Eliza Scidmore. Miss Scidmore's inclusion in this select group acknowledged the key role she played in bringing the trees to Washington.

Eliza Ruhamah Scidmore (1856–1928) was a traveler, writer and photographer who had a great love of Japan and the Japanese. She made her first trip to Japan in 1885 and spent nearly three years overall in what she called "the Island Empire," visiting her brother who held a consular position at Nagasaki, and coming away with an abiding interest in the "fascinating people and their lovely home." Her own feeling was expressed in an "Ancient Japanese Poem" which she included on the title page of her book, *Jinrikisha Days in Japan*:

> *In the ancient Yamato island, my native land, the sun rises:*
> *Must not even the western foreigner reverence?*

A native of Madison, Wisconsin, Eliza Scidmore (pronounced "SID-more") attended Oberlin College in 1873-74. In Washington, D.C., she wrote about the capital's society for out-of-town newspapers. She also served the National Geographic Society in several capacities, including as a member of its board of management. Eliza Scidmore's extensive travels throughout the Japanese archipelago, Alaska, India, China and Indonesia reflected her keen appreciation of nature's beauty and the richness of other cultures, and resulted in several other books.

A Wisconsin native, Eliza Scidmore was an intrepid traveler, writer, and photographer. Her perseverance and determination helped lead to the planting of Japanese cherry trees in Potomac Park. She died in Geneva, Switzerland, and her ashes were interred in Yokohama at the request of the Japanese government.

Her enthusiasm for the Japanese and Japan extended to include their favorite flower. As she herself wrote, "No other flower in all the world is so beloved, so exalted, so worshipped, as *sakura-no-hana*, the cherry-blossom of Japan . . . the vernal celebration of which has been observed with unflagging zeal for at least two thousand years."

Beginning with her return from her first trip to Japan in 1885, Eliza met with successive

In 1897, Congress designated 723 acres of flatlands reclaimed from the Potomac River as a public park "for the recreation and scenic pleasure of the people." The banks of the Tidal Basin and Potomac Park would later prove ideal for Japanese cherry trees.

This postcard of cherry trees in bloom in Japan is one of four from David Fairchild shown to Mrs. Taft to garner her support for planting the trees in Washington. Eliza Scidmore showed a succession of Superintendents of Public Buildings and Grounds similar postcards.

Superintendents of Public Buildings and Grounds, showing them her photographs and postcards of what she called the "most beautiful thing in the world—the Japanese Cherry Tree," hoping to convince them to plant "something of spring beauty down in the waste space . . . the great stretch of raw, reclaimed ground by the riverbank."

Her efforts were unsuccessful and she began to develop a new idea of asking for annual one-dollar subscriptions from anyone she knew or could think of who had seen the trees blooming in Japan. Her goal was to be able to give 100 trees every year, and in ten years there would be 1000 trees blooming in Potomac Park.

Before she could embark on this plan, President William Howard Taft was inaugurated on March 4, 1909, and Helen Herron Taft became First Lady with a goal to improve the city of Washington. After she received a letter on April 5 requesting her help to plant cherry trees in Potomac Park, her reply was swift and affirmative:

The White House, Washington
My Dear _____:
Thank you very much for your suggestion about the cherry trees. I have taken the matter up and am promised the trees, but thought perhaps it would be best to make an avenue of them extending to the turn of the road, as the other part (beyond the railroad bridge.—Ed) is still too rough to do any planting. Of course they could not reflect in the water, but the effect would be lovely on the long avenue. Let me know what you think about this.
Sincerely yours, HELEN H. TAFT
April 7, 1909

27

Eliza Scidmore was not alone in her efforts to promote the use of Japanese flowering cherry trees in American landscapes. Dr. David Grandison Fairchild (1869–1954) and his wife, Marian "Daisy" Bell Fairchild (1880–1962), were acquaintances of hers and also enthusiastic proponents of the beautiful trees.

As an official Plant Explorer of the U.S. Department of Agriculture, Dr. Fairchild traveled around the world, looking for plants that could be imported in the U.S. to improve crops, limit the nation's reliance on external sources, and expand ornamental choices. Fairchild sought to improve the plant selection available in the U.S. both through the introduction of existing species and through the cross-breeding of different varieties to enhance the characteristics of plants available for commercial use. Some of the plants he helped introduce to America are the Chinese soy bean, pistachios, nectarines, bamboo, avocados and mangoes.

Fairchild and his wife, Marian, a daughter of Alexander Graham Bell, planted 25 twenty-five different varieties of imported Japanese cherry trees as an experiment at their Maryland home, called "In the Woods." The trees—planted to form a *sakura-michi* or cherry path, and a *sakura-no* or cherry field shielded by pines and cedars—were successful, and the Fairchilds began to actively promote the planting of the trees throughout the Washington area. Their efforts led to an order for 300 trees by the Chevy Chase Land Company for plantings along the streets of its development, and another order for 300 trees by Mrs. Thomas Walsh to be planted at "Friendship," her Washington city estate. They themselves gave 150 trees to be planted in the school yard of every public school in the District of Columbia.

School boys from each school were chosen to visit "In the Woods" on Arbor Day, 1908, to receive the

The 125 blossoming cherry trees the Fairchilds imported from Yokohama Nurseries in Japan included 25 different varieties, and most thrived in the Washington area's growing conditions, creating the "sakuro-no" or field of cherries at "In the Woods" they had hoped for. It was Marian's idea to plant them along the Speedway.

trees. They were to bring twine and burlap, and were given a tree and planting instructions to take back to their schools. The next day, Dr. Fairchild spoke at the Franklin School when its cherry tree was to be planted in Franklin Park, across from the school building. In his illustrated lecture, he presented the idea of about Japanese cherry trees and have made something of a study of them. Every time we have driven on the Speedway Mrs. Fairchild has brought up a favorite plan of hers, which is to present the Speedway with fifty selected Japanese flowering cherry trees . . . The location lends itself peculiarly to the fairylike effects which these trees produce near watersides. The trees come into bloom at just the right time in Spring when everybody is thinking of the outdoor world."

Having shown the pictures to Mrs. Taft, Cosby responded to Fairchild, accepting his offer. He noted that Mrs. Taft had already directed the purchase of Japanese cherry trees from Hoopes and Company, a Philadelphia nursery, but the Fairchilds' trees were presumed to be more "choice."

David Fairchild and his colleague, P.H. Dorsett (standing), explored the world looking for plants that would enhance American agricultural products and landscape choices. Although a worldwide traveler, Fairchild never saw the cherry trees in bloom in Japan.

transforming the Speedway area of Potomac Park, saying "here is where thousands of Japanese flowering cherry trees should be planted." Eliza Scidmore was present at his invitation, and it was his goal to support her longstanding dream of seeing Japanese cherry trees blooming throughout the new park.

In April of the following year, the idea of planting Japanese cherry trees was revived and Fairchild wrote to Spencer Cosby, the new Superintendent of Buildings and Grounds, enclosing four color images of the trees in bloom in Japan:

"You know Mrs. Fairchild and I are quite crazy

Often called weeping or drooping, Higan cherry trees are the earliest blooming variety of Japanese ornamental cherry trees, and were the variety given by the Fairchilds for school boys to plant in Washington's school yards in 1908.
YAEBENISHIDARE,
Prunus Pendula
"Plena-rosea"

29

First Lady and the Mayor

By all accounts, First Lady Helen Herron Taft, widely known as "Nellie," shared her husband's intellectual interests and was admired for her own talents and abilities. A native of Cincinnati, Ohio, she taught school there and also served as President of the Cincinnati Symphony Orchestra. She visited the White House as a guest of President and Mrs. Hayes when she was seventeen years old, a thrilling experience she never forgot. She married William Howard Taft in 1886, and encouraged her husband in his legal and political career, including several judgeships and a stint as Solicitor General of the United States before he agreed to take charge of the American civil government of the Philippines in 1900.

Nellie Taft and their three children moved to Manila to be with him. While there, Nellie enjoyed the drive along the Luneta, a riverside park with a tree-lined pool and a view of Manila Bay. She thought a similar feature would enhance Washington, then about to begin to undergo the urban development called for by the McMillan Commission and its Burnham Plan of 1902, which restored and improved upon Charles L'Enfant's 1791 plan for the city. Mrs. Taft also visited Japan, living for several months in Yokohoma and spending a summer in Chiuzenji.

The Tafts returned to Washington in 1904 when he was appointed Secretary of War, a position which included oversight of the Army Corps of Engineers, which was responsible for reclaiming and improving the land now known as Potomac Park in addition to other changes being made to the nation's capital in accordance with the Burnham Plan. As Secretary, Taft took a personal interest in these developments, likely with Nellie's strong support.

Shortly after Taft's inauguration as President in March 1909, Nellie Taft used her new position and influence as First Lady to support the idea of planting Japanese cherry trees along the roadsides and the river banks of the new Potomac

Helen Herron Taft (1861–1943) was known for her abilities and strong intellect. She was a compelling force behind the planting of Japanese cherry trees in Washington, D.C., and on March 27, 1912, she planted the first one of the more than 3,000 given by Japan.

The "Speedway," now known as Potomac Drive thanks to Mrs. Taft, was a bleak stretch of road in 1908 used for carriage drives where the maximum "speed" was fifteen miles per hour. The distinctive railway bridge across the Potomac is visible in the background.

One of four evocative photographs of cherry trees blooming along waterways in Japan, enclosed in a letter from David Fairchild and shown to Helen Taft, offering a gift of fifty Japanese cherry trees to be planted in Potomac Park.

Park. Prior to any notion of a gift of the trees from Japan, Mrs. Taft requested that cherry trees be ordered from an American nursery and planted in Potomac Park and authorized the acceptance of a gift of fifty trees from the Fairchilds.

Her direct involvement is clear from a memo sent by the Landscape Gardener at the time, George Brown, to the Superintendent of Public Buildings and Grounds: "Mrs. Taft desires, if practicable, pre- sent plantings of Japan flowering cherries bordering [the] road from the inlet to the Tidal Basin to the park boundary northward (either in rows or in groups) so as to form masses, or continuous lines of bright color in the spring and early summer months when these trees bloom."

Sadly, Nellie Taft suffered a stroke in May of 1909 and she spent the next two years recovering. The task of fulfilling her desires fell to others.

31

Cherry Trees Arrive in Washington

Helen Taft's interest in planting Japanese cherry trees in Potomac Park became publicly known, probably through the efforts of Eliza Scidmore and her well-established Japanese connections. A New York chemist and Japanese native, Dr. Jokichi Takamine, renowned for his work on adrenaline and other patents, offered to donate 2,000 trees to the city of Washington as a gift from the city of Tokyo. Takamine wanted to make the gift through the city because it would have appeared inappropriate for a private individual to make such a gift then. Eliza herself returned to Japan in May of 1909 and interceded with Yokohama Nurseries regarding shipments of other plants requested through David Fairchild. She likely played a role in helping the Japanese arrange the gift of the cherry trees.

On August 30, 1909, an official letter from Japan notified the U.S. Department of State that the city of Tokyo intended to donate cherry trees to the United States:

" . . .the news that the planting of Japanese cherry trees along the Potomac Drive of the City of Washington is contemplated having reached Japan, the city of Tokyo, prompted by a desire to show its friendly sentiments towards its sister Capital City of the United States, has decided to offer as a gift two thousand young trees raised in Japan." The gift also had national overtones, expressing Japan's gratitude for America's role in negotiating the peace treaty ending the Russo-Japanese War of 1904–1905, signed at a conference hosted by President Theodore Roosevelt in Portsmouth, N.H. in 1905.

The gift was accepted, and as Washington prepared to receive the trees, the excitement must have been

Upon their arrival, the flowering cherry trees were examined by expert scientists at the Department of Agriculture's Garden Storehouse on the Washington Monument Grounds.

palpable. Even President Taft was involved, personally directing the removal in November 1909 of recently planted elms to make room for the new cherry trees.

On December 15, 1909, the 2,000 trees were shipped from Yokohama on the steamship *Kaga Maru*, destined for Seattle where they would be loaded onto refrigerated rail cars arranged by David Fairchild for their trip across the continent. They arrived in Washington on January 6, 1910, and were inspected immediately, revealing major problems. Fairchild reported on January 8 that the trees were large and their roots had been severely pruned, making their survival questionable. He later said that he had advised Eliza Scidmore that young, small trees would be preferable to large, established ones but suspected that his advice was ignored because she wanted the trees ready to display their blooms. He had the trees "topped," cut off as close as possible to the trunk, so

The trees and their wrappings were burned at the end of January 1910, after a thorough examination revealed that they were infested beyond saving with root gall worms, Chinese Diaspis scale, wood-boring insects, and other plant diseases.

that the lack of spreading branches would match the lack of roots and promote their chances for survival.

Other Department of Agriculture inspectors also examined the trees thoroughly as part of a new effort to monitor all plants introduced into the United States to prevent the spread of harmful pests and diseases. Their reports were unanimous, citing a long list of infections and infestations harbored in the trees, and the Secretary of Agriculture demanded that the trees and their wrappings be burned.

Everyone involved was aware of the potential embarrassment and difficulty such an action might evoke. Apologetic letters and messages were sent through appropriate channels with Colonel Cosby writing to Tokyo Mayor Yukio Ozaki, and the Secretary of State expressing the dismay and regret of the President and Mrs. Taft in an official letter to the Ambassador of Japan.

After receiving the consent of President Taft, Colonel Cosby ordered the trees burned on January 28, and on January 29 the Head Gardener, Charles Henlock, reported:

"Your order to destroy, by burning, the Japanese cherry trees recently received from Japan has been carried out. Not only has every particle of the trees been burned, but also the bamboo canes and the wrapping materials with which they were packed . . . The cherry trees were disposed of as follows:

1794 destroyed by order of Col. Cosby
200 destroyed at request of Dr. Howard [Chief Entomologist at the Department of Agriculture]
6 delivered to Agricultural Department, by order of Colonel Cosby.

Total number accounted for 2000."

Fairchild and other Department of Agriculture experts agreed that older trees had been sent to create a showy blossom display, while younger, smaller trees would have arrived in better health, and would have been more likely to survive.

33

A newspaper article in the *Evening Star* on January 29, 1910, mentions that "about a dozen" of the "buggiest trees" were saved for further study, and "planted out in the experimental plot of the bureau." Today, the Chief Horticulturist of the National Park Service looks out his office window and sees eighteen cherry trees planted in "nursery rows" on the Hains Point golf course, and wonders if it is possible that some trees from the first gift survive. There are no official records of their planting though they appear to be about the same age as trees known to have arrived from Japan in 1912, and their shape has the appearance of being "topped" as Fairchild directed rather than pruned into a "scaffold" shape typical for cherry trees. Could Henlock have miscounted? Were more than six kept by the Department of Agriculture? The truth of the first trees' fate and the origins of the trees on the golf course may never be known.

Intriguingly, the same article mentions that preparations were underway already in Tokyo for a new shipment of scrubbed and disinfected younger trees "able to pass quarantine."

In any case both Americans and Japanese suffered sharp disappointment after the burning of the first gift of 2,000 cherry trees. Colonel Cosby took a small step toward fulfilling Mrs. Taft's vision of a grove of the trees in Potomac Park by ordering and planting eighty ornamental cherry trees from a nursery in Rochester, New York, in April 1910. The Japanese were determined to succeed, however, and both Dr. Takamine and Mayor Ozaki committed themselves to fulfilling their original promise.

By December 1910 there were rumors in the American press confirming that another gift of trees was planned, and in fact in Japan preparations were underway to prepare 6,000 trees for shipment to the

Mayor Ozaki visited Washington in 1931 with his daughter and a friend, and saw in person the results of his persistence and determined efforts to have Japanese cherry trees given to the city.

United States: 3000 to be sent as a gift to Washington, D.C., as a gift from the city of Tokyo, as before, and 3,000 to go to New York City as a gift from the Japanese Society there.

Mayor Ozaki wrote Colonel Cosby on February 2, 1912, to confirm the gift, saying: "it gives [the people of this city] boundless pleasure to think that the trees may in a measure add to the embellishment of your magnificent capital.

As for the first lot of trees which we sent you three years ago, we are more than satisfied that you dealt with them as you did; for it would have pained us endlessly to have them remain a permanent source of trouble. The present trees have been raised under the spe-

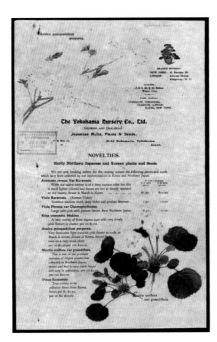

A price list on rice paper from the Yokohama Nursery Company features cherry blossoms in its upper left-hand corner, demonstrating the importance of the ornamental trees to the company's trade.

cial care of scientific experts and are reasonably expected to be free from the defects of their predecessors."

To that end, a committee of Japanese experts was formed at the Okitsu Imperial Horticultural Experiment Station. This group chose and propagated select specimens of ornamental cherry trees from the Ekita-mura area along the banks of the Arakawa River that they believed would travel well and thrive in their new environment. By the end of January 1912, the trees were ready for shipment to the U.S. The Director of the Nishigahara Agricultural Station in Tokyo outlined the precautions that had been taken to prepare the new shipment of trees, including using a field of virgin soil, free from nematode infection,

Colonel Spencer Cosby

Colonel Spencer Cosby (1868–1962) was a Baltimore native who graduated as a "first" from West Point. His forty-one year career in the U.S. Army Corps of Engineers included assignments in the Philippines and Paris, France, during World War I in addition to his posting to Washington, D.C.

He contributed in many ways to the improvements to Washington, beyond the planting of the Japanese cherry trees. He supervised the dredging of Potomac Flats to reclaim the land which became Potomac Park, and the installation of filtration plants that gave Washington mud-free water. Cosby also oversaw the design and construction of new executive offices at the White House, including a new office for President Taft, later known as the Oval Office.

At that time, the Officer in charge of Public Buildings and Grounds also served as the Chief Military Aide to the President. He supervised the junior military or assistant aides selected by the President, detailing and scheduling their duties. He also was responsible for special events and presented guests to the President and First Lady at functions.

Late in his life, Cosby proudly recalled how prophetic he was when he wrote to Mayor Ozaki in 1912 after the trees were planted: "The trees completely surround the Tidal Basin and, when in bloom in the spring, will make a magnificent display which can be seen from any part of the roads or walks which run around the Basin. In a few years this will undoubtedly be one of the famous sights of Washington, and a constant reminder to our citizens of the kindly feeling of your City and Country."

35

Washington landmarks including the Japanese cherry trees dotting the banks of the Tidal Basin and roadways of Potomac Park are visible in this 1923 U.S. Army Air Service photograph. The Navy's "Temporary" World War I office buildings north of the Reflecting Pool were not removed until 1971— when they were replaced by Constitution Gardens.

taking the specimens from a disease-free location, and using fumigation, fungicides and insecticides effectively.

The trees left Japan on the steamship *Awa Maru*, transported free of charge as had been done for the first gift. Also as before, official wheels turned in Washington and a special agent of the Department of Agriculture was designated to meet the ship when it arrived on March 13, 1912 and to accept the trees before shipping them across the country in temperature-controlled rail cars once again. Customs duties were waived as they were for the first shipment.

The pro-forma that was invoice issued by the Yokohama Nursery Company, Ltd and that accompanied the trees shows company offices in New York City and London, underscoring the need for Japanese plant suppliers to establish and maintain a reputation for supplying disease and pest-free plants.

Colonel Cosby showed the packing list to Mrs.

Taft on March 6, 1912, and plans were made to plant the trees throughout Potomac Park as well as on the White House grounds and elsewhere in the city.

The trees arrived in Washington on March 26, and on March 27 the Secretary of Agriculture informed Colonel Cosby that "so far as the inspection has gone, the trees seem singularly free from injurious insects or plant diseases."

Less than a month later, Cosby wrote exuberantly to Mayor Ozaki, complimenting him on the splendid condition of the trees, and conveying the Agriculture inspectors' approval of them. He went on to describe the planting of the first tree:

"Mrs. Taft went herself to Potomac Park and planted the first tree with her own hands [on the afternoon of March 27, 1912] in the presence of the Japanese Ambassador and his wife. At the invitation of Mrs. Taft, the Viscountess Chinda planted the second tree."

The Yoshino cherry trees planted around the Tidal Basin were well-established and blooming profusely by 1915, as this photograph taken using a glass plate shows. The placement of the subtly hued Yoshino trees to reflect in the water proved an inspired choice.

Trees

A glass slide taken for the Office of the Public Buildings and Grounds prior to 1920 shows that the flourishing Japanese cherry trees were already providing inspiration and introducing the possibility of enchantment to Washington's cityscape.

Although Cosby failed to mention that he and Eliza Scidmore were also present, news accounts of the day and their reminiscences confirm their attendance. David Fairchild had pressed without success for a more elaborate occasion to counter the negative press that the first ill-fated shipment had received, but neither he nor his wife were present.

Mrs. Taft and Viscountess Chinda planted Yoshino Japanese cherry trees a few hundred yards west of the John Paul Jones statue. Memorial bronze plaques on rocks were placed near each tree in 1931, where they can be found today. One reads: "Japanese cherry, Prunus Yedoensis. A gift from the City of Tokyo. Planted March 27, 1912, by Mrs. Willam H. Taft in the presence of the Ambassador from Japan and Viscountess Chinda." The other is similar, noting that Viscountess Chinda planted a tree in the presence of Mrs. Taft.

On March 6, 1912, Colonel Cosby took the cherry trees packing list to Mrs. Taft to discuss where the trees would be planted. The blossom descriptions were added in pencil.

List of the 3020 cherry trees shipped from Japan in 1912

Quantity	Name, blossom description
1800	"Somei-Yoshino" single-pink
20	"Mikuruma-Gayeshi" light pink, single + double
130	"Shira-Yuki" single-white
350	"Kwan-zan" large double-deep pink
100	"Ari-Ake" single-white
80	"Jo-Nioi" single-white
20	"Gyo-i-kô" double-greenish white
160	"Ichiyô" large double-light pink
120	"Fugen-zô" large double-light pink
50	"Fuku-Roku-Ju" double-deep pink
140	"Taki-Nioi" single-white
50	"Surugadai-Nioi" single-white

Yoshino trees were planted around the Tidal Basin, near the Capitol Building, Library of Congress, and other public grounds and parks, and some were kept aside for future use. The Gyo-i-kô trees with their unusual green blossoms were planted on the White House grounds. Only about 100 of the original Yoshino trees survive today. The other varieties were either not hardy enough to withstand Washington's climate, or were washed away in floods.

37

Cherry Trees Enhance the Tidal Basin

Nature's beauty has inspired artists in every age and working with any media for millennia. From pictures of animals in prehistoric caves to fine art paintings of the Rockies or the Hudson River Valley, finding many artists focused on the same subject is not uncommon, especially one that is distinctive in some way and especially beautiful.

What is new, historically speaking, is the invention of photography in the early 19th century. Its widespread adoption by professionals and amateurs allowed many to capture fleeting moments in time, beyond those who are artists trained in the fine arts of painting and drawing.

Frances Benjamin Johnston (1864–1952), one of the first prominent American women photographers, created a whimsical portrait at the turn of the 20th century. She was a photojournalist and portrait photographer in her early career, later turning to gardening and architectural photography. She covered significant events and carried out various projects, including the Carnegie Survey of the Architecture of the South, a systematic visual record of early American buildings and gardens in the region undertaken between 1933 and 1940. Frances Benjamin Johnston (1864–1952), Mills Thompson, Photographic print, ca. 1890–1910.

David and Marian Bell Fairchild, early proponents of planting Japanese cherry trees in Washington, also were avid photographers. They recorded the development of the cherry trees growing on their own Maryland estate, and experimented with close-up views of the blossoms themselves.

38

A huddle of photographers and a painter chose the same vantage point to capture the cherry trees in bloom. The placement of the trees in relation to the Washington Monument and the Tidal Basin creates optimal viewing spots, and crowds still form at certain points to sketch or take photographs. Photographic print, 1909–1932.

Once the cherry trees in Washington were established, they quickly became a popular subject for artists and photographers. The curve of the Tidal Basin, leading the eye in an arc to the Washington Monument, has long been a favorite vantage point for artful views of the cloud-like masses of blooms. Many choose it because the trees and the Monument are seen equally well, the Tidal Basin reflecting both.

Photographers have also taken close-up, intimate pictures of the blossoms themselves. These reveal the delicate qualities of the flower parts and petals that seem to float effortlessly at the end of their twigs, like gossamer handkerchiefs unfurled to welcome spring.

During World War II, families reunited under the cherry blossoms as they do today, although the trees were called "oriental cherry trees" for the duration of the war. The graceful branches reaching to the water show the trees had reached mature growth and formed a flowery, arching backdrop for the photographer. Martha McMillan Roberts, Cherry Blossom Festival, *Negative nitrate, May 1941.*

39

The cherry blossoms maintain their allure and ephemeral beauty after the sun goes down, especially in the light of the moon. While the traditional Japanese "moon viewing" festival takes place in August or September, night-time images in art and poetry make it clear that viewing the blossoms in the early spring moonlight is also an important part of the Japanese experience. A poem by Basho is an excellent example:

> *The sweet spring of night*
> *Of cherry blossom viewing*
> *Has ended.*

Night-time has also been an important time for the cherry trees in Washington. The women who protested the removal of trees to make room for the Jefferson Memorial were so emphatic about their cause that the actual transplanting took place under the cover of darkness to avoid inciting them further.

In December 1941, again in the middle of the night, four large cherry trees were cut down possibly to protest the bombing of Pearl Harbor a few days earlier. The destruction of the trees was widely condemned, and the loss of their beauty deemed more important than their source. For the duration of World War II, however, they were referred to as the "oriental cherry trees."

At one time, the cherry trees surrounding the Tidal Basin were lit to enhance visitors' nocturnal visits to the blossoms. Now the flash of cameras lights up the nights when the blooms are at their peak, and during the National Cherry Blossom Festival® there are fireworks. Postcard.

At home in the night, an owl sees and hears everything under the moon. Its tufts of feathers are only that: its ears are lower down on its head. Its light-colored eyes hold the promise of day in the dark of night, just as the cherry blossoms portend the coming of spring. Ozawa Nankoku, (1844-?), Owl in Moonlight, *Hanging scroll, Ink and color on silk with ivory jiku, 166 x 82.3 cm overall.*

Each year, the National Cherry Blossom Festival® holds a competition for the artwork used in posters and other materials promoting the Festival, on the official Festival t-shirts, and other commemorative products. The design by Sucha Snidvongs for 2002 featured the moon in conjunction with a torii *or gateway to a Shinto shrine and the Jefferson Memorial.*

Another dangerous night for the trees occurred in 1999 when beavers felled four trees by gnawing through their trunks. Covered extensively in the media at the time, the perpetrators reportedly were trapped and moved to a wildlife area with less famous trees to chew, and that version of the story has entered into Washington area lore. The fact is that beavers still live along the Potomac River and could find their way to the cherry trees for a reprise any day, or night.

In America too, viewing cherry blossoms at night can be a peak life experience. As Maud Kay Sites wrote, "In the pale grey dawn the rosy cloud of blossoms heralds the sunrise, under the noonday sun it glows with paler radiance, and in the moonlight it is the living expression of the poet's soul."

41

Upon its completion, the Tidal Basin was used for many purposes in addition to cherry blossom viewing. A bathing beach, located approximately where the Jefferson Memorial is now that was in use from 1918 through 1925, complementing the amenities of the nearby public campground in Potomac Park. Different kinds of boats were offered for public use, including canoes, swan boats and battery-powered speed boats. Fishing was a perennial favorite.

The site for the Jefferson Memorial was chosen in 1937 as the southern-most anchor of a north-south axis with the White House, crossing the east-west line drawn between the Capitol and the Lincoln Memorial with the Washington Monument near the center. The choice was controversial because several of the Japanese cherry trees would have had to be removed to make room for the new Memorial. Local society matrons took up the cause, taking their protest to the White House and chaining themselves to the trees.

Eventually, President Franklin D. Roosevelt himself affirmed the Memorial's location and it was promised that the trees would be re-planted, not cut down. Feelings ran so high that the trees' removal was performed at night to avoid renewed public outcry.

President Franklin D. Roosevelt supported the concept of the Jefferson Memorial in spite of furious local society women distressed at the thought of losing any of the Japanese cherry trees lining the Tidal Basin. He also authorized the Memorial's classical design, shown here in 1941, and laid its cornerstone in 1939.

A swan boat plied the waters of the Tidal Basin beginning in 1926 when it was christened with milk poured by a four-year-old. Associated with the Child Welfare Board of Children's Hospital, the boat was pontoon-style with seats on a platform under a canopy, as this 1957 image shows.

The Tidal Basin was home to sail boats in the 1960s, and fine sailing weather overlapped with the cherry blossoms' peak bloom on at least one occasion. Today, paddle boats are available for hire, and a trip to the middle of the Tidal Basin provides a fresh and uncrowded view of the monuments and cherry trees.

Roosevelt also was the final arbiter regarding the Memorial's design. Architect John Russell Pope had proposed the neo-classic design, inspired by the Pantheon in Rome, as an expression of Jefferson's own architectural tastes. The Commission of Fine Arts objected because it would compete with the Lincoln Memorial. The Jefferson Memorial Commission appealed to Roosevelt, and he approved the pantheon design. Roosevelt laid the cornerstone of the Jefferson Memorial in November 1939, and the building was dedicated on April 13, 1943, the 200th anniversary of Thomas Jefferson's birth.

Today, the Jefferson Memorial is well-known for its beautiful setting amidst the blooming cherry trees each spring. In addition to performances and other activities associated with the National Cherry Blossom Festival®, the Memorial hosts a number of events and ceremonies throughout the year.

The Jefferson Memorial's setting among the Japanese cherry trees is appropriate because Thomas Jefferson was a man of many interests, including horticulture. At Monticello, his home near Charlottesville, Virginia, he grew a wide variety of native and exotic trees, and appreciated their ornamental value.

43

The timing of the cherry trees' peak bloom depends on the weather in February and March, and extreme heat or cold will speed up or delay their opening. While peak bloom can occur as early as March 15 or as late as April 18, all the trees in each variety of Japanese cherry tend to bloom at about the same time, creating an impressive display whenever it occurs.

For decades, the media in Washington have paid close attention to the buds' progress, transmitting the National Park Service Chief Horticulturist's fore-cast to a public eagerly waiting for the blossoms to open. Whatever the weather, it makes the news: snow, sleet, rain, wind, heat wave or "heavenly."

Some years, torrential rains pour down and the high waters of the Tidal Basin lap over the sidewalk, submerging the lower out-stretched limbs of some of the cherry trees and making a walk under the trees a sloppy affair. Other years, strong winds make cherry blossom viewing a short-lived option as the petals blow off the trees soon after they bloom and white

Lovers stroll under the cherry blossoms around the Tidal Basin each spring, no matter what the weather. When it's fine, they "enjoy" more company.

Snow-laden cherry blossoms display a different beauty, probably revealed only to intrepid devotees who will make a pilgrimage to admire them in any weather.

caps move across the Tidal Basin. On occasion, snow and frost also play havoc with the blossoms. In 1930, for example, the cherry trees were blooming on April 6, and on April 7 they were pummeled by a storm of rain, hail and snow, embellished with lightning and thunder.

Many years, however, the spring weather is "perfect" and everyone strolling or picnicking beneath the blooming trees shares a sense of exhilaration and joy inspired by the exquisite and exuberant blossoms. A poem by Basho expresses the feeling of awe the trees in bloom can inspire:

> *Flowers from an unknown tree*
> *Filled me with their fragrance.*

Wind tugs a photographer's skirt, her subject's tie and the blossoms off the trees in 1974 when hemlines were almost as high as the cherry trees are tall.

Clifford Berryman

Clifford Berryman (1869-1949), the political cartoonist perhaps best known for his 1902 sketch of Teddy Roosevelt choosing not to shoot a bear while hunting in Mississippi, which inspired the creation of teddy bear plush toys, was the chief cartoonist for the *Washington Evening Star* newspaper for more than thirty years.

His humor had a whimsical quality as shown in this cartoon dated April 20, 1934. Titled "Cherry blossom time in Washington!" it probably appeared in the *Evening Star* and refers to New Deal plans and legislation. Competing government interests represented by key figures associated with them pay homage to President Franklin D. Roosevelt and the leaders of the House of Representatives and Senate against a backdrop of blooming cherry trees framing the Washington Monument.

National Gifts

The 1912 gift of Japanese cherry trees spawned several later gifts between Japan and the United States. The U.S. sent dogwood trees to Japan in 1915, acknowledging the gift of the cherry trees. In 1952, the grove of cherry trees along the Arakawa River near Tokyo was in decline following World War II. It was the grove where the original trees sent to the U.S. had been cultivated, and the Japanese wanted to restore it. Bud wood from the Yoshino trees around the Tidal Basin was sent to replenish and recreate the original grove.

The Stone Lantern was given to the U.S. in 1954 on the 100th anniversary of the signing of the first Treaty of Peace, Amity and Commerce between Japan and the United States, signed by Commodore Matthew C. Perry on March 31, 1854. The granite Lantern is one of a pair that stood on the grounds of To-ei-zan Kan'eiji, a temple in the area that now forms Ueno Park in Tokyo. It is eight and a half feet high and weighs two tons. It is about 350 years old.

Each year the annual Lighting of the Lantern is a highlight of the National Cherry Blossom Festival®. The formal ceremony features traditional Japanese performers and many Washington dignitaries.

The Japanese Pagoda, a gift from the City of Yokohama in 1958, also commemorates the signing of the Treaty of 1854.

To honor First Lady Lady Bird Johnson's beautification efforts Japan gave the U.S. 3800 cherry trees in 1965 to be planted around the Washington Monument and elsewhere in the capital. Due to a prohibition against importing fruit trees imposed by the U.S. Department of Agriculture, these trees were cultivated in America.

The Mayor of Yokohama presented the rough stone Japanese Pagoda to the City of Washington in April 1958 as a symbol of the spirit of friendship between the U.S. and Japan, and to commemorate the signing of the Treaty of Peace, Amity and Commerce signed at Yokohama on March 31, 1854

In 1982, Japanese horticulturists collected about 800 cuttings from the Yoshino cherry trees around the Tidal Basin to retain the genetic characteristics of the trees and to replace some in Japan that had been lost when a river changed its course.

One hundred cherry trees were presented to President Bill Clinton by Japan's national legislature,

The Japanese Lantern standing near the two original trees planted by Mrs. Taft and Viscountess Chinda is lit once a year to signal the beginning of the National Conference of State Societies' activities associated with the National Cherry Blossom Festival®. A daughter of a Japanese diplomat assigned to Washington usually lights it.

the Diet, when he visited Japan in 1996. These were planted around the Tidal Basin and along the banks of the Potomac River in 1997 following an official ceremony including Soichiro Ito, then Speaker of the Japanese House of Representatives and President of the Japan Cherry Blossom Association.

Fifty trees propagated from the "Usuzumi" cherry tree, a National Treasure of Japan growing in Neo Mura Village in the Gifu Prefecture of Japan, were given to the U.S. in 1999 and planted in West Potomac Park. The Usuzumi tree was planted by an emperor in the 6th century, C.E., to commemorate eighteen happy years he spent there. The tree itself is known for its distinctive single blossoms, which are slightly rouged in bud form, then bloom in white and turn gray immediately before falling.

First Lady Lady Bird Johnson

Lady Bird Johnson and the wife of the Ambassador from Japan planted cherry trees on April 6, 1965, re-creating the planting of the first trees from Japan in 1912 and honoring the "second generation" gift. Because of U.S. import restrictions, the 3,800 trees were cultivated in America and many were planted around the Washington Monument.

First Lady Lady Bird Johnson (1912–) planted a cherry tree representing the "second generation" gift from Japan of 3,800 trees to the U.S. in 1965. Following the example set in 1912, the wife of the Japanese ambassador at the time, Mrs. Ryuji Takeuchi, planted a second tree. The gift of these trees honored Lady Bird's commitment to environmental issues, especially enhancing the nation's capital and highways.

Lady Bird's belief that beautiful environments improved the quality of life for all led to the establishment of a First Lady's Committee for a More Beautiful National Capital which addressed improving the areas of the city visited by tourists as well as those less prominent and dilapidated. Many of the city's parks and plantings today are the legacy of Lady Bird and the Society's work.

Nationally, Lady Bird worked to improve the views and vistas bordering the interstate highway system. She wanted unsightly billboards and junkyards removed and replaced with wildflowers and natural landscaping. The Highway Beautification Act of 1965 was developed at her behest, and passed due to the strong support of her husband, President Lyndon Baines Johnson (1908–1973).

47

National Cherry Blossom Festival

A Celebration of Spring for Over 50 Years

Crowds under the cherry blossoms enjoy the annual rite of spring in Washington, D.C., on foot as seen here, or by car or busload.

Early Fêtes and Festivals

Like the Japanese, Americans love festivals and celebrations, and Washingtonians realized early on that the blooming cherry trees were an occasion worth honoring. From the earliest fêtes and pageants, the friendship between Japan and the United States was highlighted in the program and reflected in the participants.

The earliest recorded event held to honor the cherry trees while they were blooming around the Tidal Basin was a simple re-enactment by school children in 1927 of the original 1912 tree planting. In subsequent years, a number of different types of fêtes or pageants was presented, and by 1934 the activities had expanded to three days, followed by the first crowning of a Cherry Blossom Queen in 1935.

High-ranking national political figures or media personalities frequently played important roles in the festivities. The First Lady often was a principal patron, and sometimes she even crowned the Cherry Blossom Queen.

A pageant, musical events, and sports performances were typical, and of course there usually was a parade. For a time, the parade was held at night and the "illuminated floats" must have transformed the downtown parade route lined with office blocks in the same way the cherry trees in bloom enhanced the Tidal Basin and Potomac Park.

Japanese activities and traditions were prominently featured. For example, young women related to Japanese diplomats assigned to their country's embassy in Washington have lit the granite Japanese Lantern to open the Festival, rain or shine, since its arrival commemorating the centennial of the treaty of Yeddo in 1954. First Ladies, Vice Presidents, or

The friendship between America and Japan was a theme of the earliest known festival honoring the blooming cherry trees in Washington. Held in 1927, two women clasping hands portray the "Spirit of the Cherry Flower" (right) and the "Spirit of America" (left) in a celebration of Japan's gift that helped to make the city famous as a place of beauty.

Cabinet Secretaries have assisted in lighting the Lantern, underscoring the importance of honoring the friendship between Japan and America.

In 1966, then Vice President Hubert Humphrey protected a young woman probably related to a Japanese diplomat from the rain as she gamely lit the Lantern, a signature Festival event since 1954 no matter what the weather. Her kimono features cherry blossoms with their five distinctive notched, heart-shaped petals.

The Festival was suspended during World War II, from 1942–46, and during that time the trees themselves were referred to as "Oriental Cherry Trees." The first post-war Festival was held in 1947, with a record-breaking crowd of 450,000 cramming into the Tidal Basin area in a two-day period. Clearly, the cherry blossoms and the Festival celebrating them were well-established as essential to a proper welcome to spring in Washington.

Over the years, many different activities have been held in conjunction with the Festival. A fashion show and luncheon have been held, as well as drill team competitions, water shows, and boat races.

THE 1962
NATIONAL
CHERRY BLOSSOM
FESTIVAL

LUNCHEON AND FASHION SHOW

The honorary chair of the Festival is frequently the First Lady, and a luncheon and fashion show featuring different designers have been a highlight of the events associated with the National Cherry Blossom Festival® for many years. In 1962, the honorary chair was Mrs. John F. Kennedy and the New York Couture Group was featured.

51

Parades and Princesses

The Cherry Blossom Princesses, a program of the National Conference of State Societies, are young women from every state and territory, including Washington, D.C., and from many countries overseas. The Princesses participate in the National Cherry Blossom Festival Parade® and other Festival events.

Cherry Blossom Princesses are selected on the basis of their leadership qualities, academic achieve-ments, and evidence of their interest in community and world affairs. They represent the history and traditions of their home state or territory during a week-long program of educational, leadership, and cultural activities intended to introduce them to decision-makers and role models in the Nation's Capital, to members of the international community, and to each other.

For a time in the 1950s, the National Cherry Blossom Festival Parade® was held at night, and its illuminated floats lit up Washington's darkened downtown K street, creating a magical scene, complementing and celebrating the springtime transformation of the cherry trees around the Tidal Basin.

The "Heart of Texas" float in 1966 carries the Texas Cherry Blossom Princess and her bevy of attendants, whose clear parasols are festooned with flowers, possibly yellow roses, to honor the blooming cherry trees and other signs of spring in the Nation's Capital.

Cherry Blossom Princesses participate in a variety of National Cherry Blossom Festival® activities. Princesses in 1970 check the buds for signs of growth with a National Park Service expert, their happy looks suggesting peak blooms were expected in time for the Festival itself.

Since 1948, more than 2,800 young women have participated in the Cherry Blossom Princess Program. Beginning in 1996, the diplomatic community was invited to participate in Princess Partners, strengthening and expanding the international dimension of the Princess Program.

In addition to representing their home state or territory in the National Cherry Blossom Festival Parade®, Cherry Blossom Princesses attend the Lantern Lighting Ceremony, the Congressional Reception, and the Grand Ball, among other Festival activities. The Grand Ball is a formal occasion, with a Sushi Reception and Silent Auction as well as the selection and coronation of the Cherry Blossom Queen. Each Princess wears a long white ball gown of her own choosing and long white gloves, appropriate for the gala occasion attended by dignitaries, celebrities, and members of the diplomatic community, especially Japan's Ambassador to the U.S. and his wife, and Japan's Cherry Blossom Queen.

Chosen by the Japan Cherry Blossom Association on the basis of merit and presence, Japan's Cherry Blossom Queen is one of two young women selected to serve for two years as representatives of Japan at cherry blossom-related events around the globe. They take turns attending festivals and other activities promoting Japan's friendship with many countries.

The National Conference of State Societies (NCSS) is a congressionally chartered association of State Societies that are nonpartisan social and civic clubs in the National Capital area, providing venues for out-of-towners to celebrate and maintain connections with their home state or territory, and to build relationships across home state and political lines.

The Cherry Blossom Queen's crown is a treasured work of art made of 1,585 pearls and 14k gold. Given to Festival officials in 1957 as a gesture of friendship by the Mikimoto Company, it took the firm's jewelers nearly two months to create. The Queen wears it only briefly because of its great weight.

The selection and coronation of the Cherry Blossom Queen take place during the Grand Ball and Banquet hosted by the National Conference of State Societies (NCSS). A giant wheel of fortune is spun, and the Princess of the state indicated where its tickler stops becomes the Cherry Blossom Queen. Preferring chance over other possible criteria to select the Queen maintains the focus of the Princess Program on learning experiences and relationship building, which the NCSS seeks to foster through its Cherry Blossom Festival activities.

In 1962, however, the wheel of fortune proved fickle, and after stopping at Colorado, it moved on to Rhode Island. One Princess was the daughter of a lieutenant governor, the other a daughter of a senator. After what must have been several awkward moments, Festival officials named both Princesses co-Queens.

After her coronation, the Cherry Blossom Queen reigns for a full year. She rides on a special float in the National Cherry Blossom Festival Parade® with the Japanese Cherry Blossom Queen and Princess, and the Dogwood Queen from Japan, and participates in other Cherry Blossom Festival and NCSS activities. A highlight of her duties is a trip to Japan as the guest of the Japan Cherry Blossom Association. She meets with dignitaries and others to expand cultural awareness and understanding as a representative of the U.S. and her home state.

The 2003 Cherry Blossom Queen, Elizabeth Krabill, wore the gold and pearl crown tied with black satin ribbons beneath her chin in order to secure it to her head while photos were taken. The unique crown is kept in a bank vault during the year between Festivals, and special guards protect it during the Gala.

A Cherry Blossom Queen points to her home state of Wyoming where the tickler stopped on the wheel of fortune in 1951. Every year since 1948, the selection of the Cherry Blossom Queen has been left purely to chance, and the winning Princess enjoys the random stroke of good luck.

Cherry Blossom Queens meet with high-level officials, often heads of state, during their year-long reign. In 1984, Ronald Reagan greeted the Cherry Blossom Queen and Princesses in the White House Rose Garden as welcome and traditional signs of spring in Washington after a long winter.

As a living reminder and a tangible gesture of friendship between Japan and the U.S., the Cherry Blossom Queen plants American dogwood and cherry trees at many locations she visits in Japan.

The Cherry Blossom Queen's Official Crown is another gift honoring the friendship between Japan and the U.S. Given to Festival officials in 1957 by Yoshitaka Mikimoto, president of the Mikimoto Company, the crown was created by the firm's skilled craftsmen and jewelers from pearls hand-chosen by Mr. Mikimoto himself. The crown features 1,585 pearls ranging in size from three millimeters to a large eighteen-millimeter Mabe pearl. The crown's pearl-topped fronds and other scroll and leaf decorations are finely worked in 14k gold and its base is ringed with pearls above a band of ermine.

The crown is so heavy, it must be tied securely to her head with wide black satin ribbons, and the Queen can wear it only long enough to permit a few photo opportunities. For the remainder of the Ball and other Festival activities, she wears a much smaller replica, just as the Japanese Cherry Blossom Queen wears a replica of the Japanese crown. Both Queens keep the replicas as mementos and also receive cultured pearl necklaces by Mikimoto as commemorative gifts.

Being crowned Cherry Blossom Queen is literally the chance of a lifetime, and it provides an unforgettable and thrilling experience for the lucky Princess whose home state is where the wheel of fortune stops.

55

The National Cherry Blossom Festival Parade® is a signature event of the two-week-long Festival. Marching bands and drill teams typical of many all-American parades share the limelight with performers, drummers and dancers from Japan and other countries from around the world in a celebration of global friendship and the coming of spring.

The Cherry Blossom Princesses are among the Parade's leaders, walking the distance of the route accompanied by their home state, territory, or national flag. The cherry tree maintenance crew and their tree trimmer truck form part of the parade along with celebrities, dignitaries, clowns, performing cowboys, bagpipers, international folk dance or ritual performers, many bands, and drill teams. Huge overhead balloons are pulled along the parade route, interspersed between the floats and other participants. The overall effect is exciting and full of surprises as each new group or act comes into view.

Designed to appeal to a broad spectrum of people, the parade draws a big crowd of spectators, including local Washingtonians and national and international visitors, and jostling for sidewalk viewing space is competitive. Many opt for grandstand seats, and part of the proceeds from their ticket sales support youth charities through the Downtown Jaycees.

A highlight of the National Cherry Blossom Festival Parade® is the appearance of the newly crowned Cherry Blossom Queen with the Cherry Blossom and Dogwood Queens and a Cherry Blossom Princess from Japan on a blossom-covered pink and white float.

Rickshaws that are pedaled rather than pulled travel in circles the length of the parade route, adding a zesty interlude and a memento of old Japan between the marching bands and floats.

Elmo and balloons of other familiar characters skim above the street, adding humor to the sense of awe and wonder that their enormous size creates. Volunteers from throughout the metropolitan Washington area handle the balloons and assist with other Parade and Festival activities.

Colorful Japanese-style pennants festooned with cherry blossoms or stripes in shades of pink punctuate the array of marching bands, dancers, drummers, floats, balloons and other entertaining performers that make up the National Cherry Blossom Parade® each spring.

57

The tall, striped pennants following the Akron Tigers Marching Band of Akron, N.Y., are typical Japanese style, and are carried between different sections of the National Cherry Blossom Festival Parade® to add a Japanese flourish. The Daisy balloon is both held by wires and "walked" by people inside its two "legs," causing it to lurch and stagger up the parade route to hilarious effect.

In addition to rhythmic drumming to accompany precision marchers and to awe its listeners, music of every type is performed by bands that compete for the honor to participate in the National Cherry Blossom Festival Parade®. They submit videos of their past performances to the Festival Parade organizer and are selected based on the quality of their music, marching discipline and overall presentation. Like all the participants in the Festival, they pay their own way to Washington through fundraising activities in their home towns.

Some marching bands are accompanied by dancers and other performers, while other dancers in colorful costumes from different parts of the country and from other nations perform traditional folk dances which typically celebrate the coming of spring. Their flower-bedecked garb reflects the universal cheer that greets the end of winter.

Clowns too add a silly touch of humor to the procession as they skitter between the bands marching with military precision, under the enormous balloons overhead, and around the many other Parade participants. Prancing and dancing in their own imaginative style, they tease and joke with onlookers as well as marchers, leaving laughter in their wake.

Clowns tease and amuse spectators and parade participants alike. This cheerful, cherry-themed duo skipped and cavorted along the parade route in 2004, and the reverse of the Cherry Shake sign read "It's All Fruitless."

The opportunity to perform in the high-profile and internationally renowned National Cherry Blossom Festival Parade® is much sought after, and school bands and others who wish to be included compete for the limited number of openings in the Parade line up.

Left: Many of the Parade's performers demonstrate traditional dances celebrating spring in their native costumes like these dancers from Bolivia. Their vivid colors and dynamic motion add foot-tapping gusto to the Parade, complementing the sharp rhythms and precision performances of the marching bands and drummers.

Below: Proud to represent the Parade's host city, the Marching Knights from Washington's own Frank W. Ballou High School shimmy and strut the length of the parade route in uniquely dynamic style.

To many spectators, the appearance of an unruly crowd carrying an ornate, peak-roofed box on poles above their heads, careening from curb to curb in the midst of the orderly procession of Princesses, floats and marching bands in the National Cherry Blossom Festival Parade® is startling. To the Japanese, however, seeing the mayhem and perhaps participating in it makes them feel right at home.

Called a *mikoshi*, the five-foot gilded and decorated cube is a portable shrine. No Japanese *matsuri* or festival would be complete without one. Since the original purpose of any *matsuri* was to invite the presence and blessing of the divine or *kami* into the community, the *mikoshi* became the *kami's* home while it was transported from its permanent shrine to its temporary one for the duration of the *matsuri*.

Carried by dozens of shouting people, the portable shrine is jounced up and down as the bearers energetically swerve from side to side in a vaguely forward direction. The power of the *kami* is jolted into action by the commotion, spreading its divinity wherever it goes, bringing good health, good fortune, and protection to everyone and everything in its vicinity, and binding the community together.

Mikoshi bearers and other *matsuri* participants wear *happi* coats, similar to jackets worn by workmen. The festival jackets differ from the commercial ones, though, because the inscriptions on the lapels and the symbols on the back identify them as members of a group or shrine neighborhood rather than as a representative of a business.

Seen beyond a torii *or open gateway at the Shinto shrine of Atsuta in Nagoya, Japan, rival teams at a matsuri nearly 200 years ago display the same energy and focus that mikoshi bearers and* taiko *drummers show when they participate in the National Cherry Blossom Festival Parade® in the 21st century. Ando Hiroshige (1797–1858),* The Fifty-three Stations of Tokaido, Miya (Station 42), Festival at Atsuta Shrine, *c. 1833–34, Woodblock print, 222.25 x 3406.08 mm.*

A crowd of mikoshi *bearers lift the large and heavy portable shrine up and down as they jostle their way along Constitution Avenue in Washington, D.C., during the National Cherry Blossom Festival Parade® in 2004. In place of* happi *coats, many wear long-sleeved official Festival t-shirts.*

Known for fast and electrifying rhythms, taiko *is a popular style of drumming in Japan and in the U.S. Sometimes,* taiko *(fat drum) performers live and study in a community to better unite their spirits with the drums and with each other. In 2004,* taiko *drummers came from Zentsuji, Japan, to perform in the Parade.*

Wearing a *happi* coat as a *matsuri* participant promotes camaraderie, and implies a commitment and dedication to involvement in the festival. *Happi* coats can be worn open or wrapped closed with a thin obi, and everyone in a group will follow the same style. They also will have similar leg wear and foot gear.

The sweatbands used by *mikoshi* bearers and other *matsuri* teams are called *hachimaki*, created from a cotton towel or *tengui*, which can be twisted, folded, rolled, or knotted in many different ways. The style of wrapping can refer to a specific task or a particular figure in folklore, and it further distinguishes members of one group from other *matsuri* participants. Like the *happi* coat, wearing a *hachimaki* indicates intent to exert strenuous effort.

Generic hachimachi *or sweatbands and* happi *coats, like uniforms or jackets, were available to participants and spectators at the National Cherry Blossom Festival in 2004.*

More than a method for steeping leaves in hot water, the Japanese tea ceremony, *chanoyu*, is an expression of the Way of tea or *Chado*, and visitors to the Cherry Blossom Festival can enjoy an introduction to it. In addition to prescribed patterns for preparing food and the tea itself, the Way of tea encompasses architectural principles, garden design, ceramics, flower arranging, calligraphy, and religious thought. Its specific activities include enjoying a bowl of special tea, appreciating nature and the changing seasons, celebrating things shared, and transcending differences. Sometimes a form of meditation, it also can be simply a way to relax among friends and family.

Based on rituals imported from Chinese Zen Buddhist temples, the tea ceremony was practiced in Japan by the 8th century, C.E., and became widespread during the Heian Period (794–1185). Many aspects of the tea ceremony as it is today are attributed to

Practitioners of the tea ceremony strive to create a serene environment and tranquil mood where minds can meet and be refreshed based on rituals established in Chinese Buddhist temples. In 2004, a server prepared to make tea from a leaf-green powder called matcha, *stirred to a froth like espresso with a small whisk.*

Japanese students of Chado, the "Way of tea," prepared and presented tea following the prescribed steps of a tea ceremony at the Arthur M. Sackler Gallery as part of the National Cherry Blossom Festival in 2004. Red and white hangings, typical of Shinto rituals, provided privacy for the food preparers

Sen no Rikyu (1522–91), whose use of everyday objects and other refinements made the Way of tea accessible to common people who began to follow it in droves. There are many schools of tea today, each teaching self-discipline and promoting practices that encourage serenity.

The tea ceremony itself progresses from formal to less formal and can take up to four hours. The ideal setting, involving a teahouse and its garden, is designed to help shift attention from everyday living to the world of tea. The tea itself is prepared and presented in a prescribed ritual, and the food and flowers are appropriate for the season.

Reminiscent of scenes found on ancient screens and scrolls, an image from a stereograph about 1902 shows two young girls enjoying tea on a platform under blooming cherry trees. The tea Japanese people drink daily is made from leaves steeped in hot water.

Sakura Matsuri

Once a free-standing event of the Japanese-America Society of Washington, D.C., the *Sakura Matsuri* now is held in conjunction with the National Cherry Blossom Festival® each spring. Several downtown city blocks are transformed into a Japanese street festival to honor the blooming cherry trees, and many Japanese arts and activities are featured.

Visitors to the *Sakura Matsuri* in Washington can sample Japanese food and beer, enjoy art and craft demonstrations, readings of Japanese children's fairy tales and legends, and performances of Japanese dances, music, martial arts and sports. City dwellers and visitors alike search the tents and pavilions, following their noses to find freshly prepared and grilled Japanese specialties, and using their eyes and ears to discover new entertainments and learning adventures the *Sakura Matsuri* offers.

The Japanese food is typical of what you would find at a street fair in Japan. Some examples are: sushi and yakitori, soba noodles, *ika geso* or deep fried shrimp and calamari, *shumai* dumplings on a skewer, *futomaki* or giant vegetable rolls, along with tradition-

Held in view of the U.S. Capitol, Washington's Sakura Matsuri *gathers Japanese food, activities and entertainment in one place for the enjoyment and education of visitors and residents alike.*

Sakura Matsuri *visitors enjoy popular Japanese treats such as freshly grilled chicken yakitori and mochi, a chewy rice cake eaten with cheese or soy sauce, as well as traditional American fare like grilled corn on the cob and funnel cakes*

al bento boxes featuring Japanese picnic fare, *mochi* and other sweets.

One of the sweets you might find is named after the cherry blossom. Called *sakura-mochi*, it is a plump pink ball of rice, filled with bean jam and wrapped in cherry leaves.

And just as you would find them in Japan, premier cooks and sushi chefs join with ordinary grillers and food preparers in the street fair tents. Each contributes the best of their skills to ensure a successful *matsuri* for the community.

As a reminder of the *Sakura Matsuri's* Washington location and to ensure the enjoyment of all, traditional American food such as corn on the cob, funnel cakes and ice cream is available. Reflecting the melting pot quality of American culture, other Asian cuisines are included also, such as Chinese and Thai.

Artful flowers emerge from fresh vegetables carved by chefs trained in the art of Mukimono, a Japanese garnishing style. Red peppers inside-out become lilies and radishes are carved into roses. A competition is held during the Festival for Mukimono students and professionals to showcase their skills.

Sushi chefs from Japan come to the United States during the National Cherry Blossom Festival® for special demonstrations and taste testing of their highly refined skills of combining rice, fresh raw fish and wasabi, a green and very hot horseradish, served in small pieces and accompanied by slivers of pickled ginger

Many of the traditional Japanese games and art forms featured during the *Sakura Matsuri* were introduced to Japan from China. Ikebana or flower arranging, calligraphy, and the game of Go are examples of Japanese activities with Chinese origins.

Ikebana was introduced to Japan with Buddhism in the 6th century, C.E. Its earliest practitioners were priests who arranged flowers as offerings or decorations for religious purposes. Vessels and containers for the flowers were important features of the arrangements from the beginning in Japan, and shapes, styles and materials were developed for specific purposes, especially for use in the Tea Ceremony.

Practiced by accomplished men and women, ikebana arrangements symbolize the relationships between humankind, the heavens, and the Earth. Each arrangement typically includes several different types of plants, and features leaves and flowerless branches as well as blossoms.

Also in the 6th century, C.E., Chinese characters were adopted by the Japanese, forming the basis of the Kanji script, one of three used in Japan today. Kanji are ideograms used for nouns, verbs, adjectives and adverbs. The other two scripts, Hiragana and Katakana, are based on syllables and were developed in the 9th century to supplement Kanji.

Hiragana is simpler and more rounded than Kanji, and is the one first learned by school children. Katakana is more angular and is used for borrowed, non-Japanese words, some place names and names of people.

Calligraphy, the art of writing letters beautifully, is taught to Japanese school children, and many adults continue to enjoy it as a hobby and way to focus and still the mind. Special brushes and thin paper are used, and some make ink from scratch. The strokes of each character must be laid down in a specific order in one of three styles: square or *Kaisho*, semi-cursive or *Gyosho*, or cursive, called *Sosho*.

Demonstrations of Japanese calligraphy are offered at the Sakura Matsuri *and other National Cherry Blossom Festival® events. An art form and for some a meditative practice, Japanese letter forms are primarily derived from the Chinese writing system.*

"Go," similar to checkers, is a complex game of strategy played with black and white stones. At the Sakura Matsuri, *experts teach novices nuances of the game, and a "Go" competition is held as part of the Festival.*

The latter two styles are quicker to write and are used more often in Japan.

The board game, "Go," was introduced to Japan from China in the 8th century, C.E. Two players vie for control of territory on the board using black or white stones respectively. Through strategic moves, the players surround and "kill" their opponent's stones. The player who captures the most territory wins.

Ikebana, the Japanese art of flower arranging, uses different kinds of natural elements and man-made materials in addition to flowers to symbolize the relationship between the Earth, the heavens, and humankind. Ikebana evolved into a high art as a complement to the Tea Ceremony, and its practitioners include men and women.

67

Flaunting their impressive strength and skill at a demonstration during the 2004 Sakura Matsuri *in Washington, enormous sumo wrestlers from Japan face each other in a temporary ring that is the regulation diameter of 4.55 meters, not quite fifteen feet across.*

Sumo, a kind of wrestling, is Japan's national sport. Derived from ancient performances dedicated to the Shinto gods, sumo is said to be more than 1,500 years old. The huge wrestlers, called *rikishi* or "gentlemen of strength," belong to teams who live and train together in "stables" led by a coach.

Each sumo match is brief, lasting only several seconds, rarely as long as a minute. The object is to force the opponent out of the ring or make any part of his body other than the soles of his feet touch the floor. Punching, gouging, or pulling hair is not permitted though pushing, tripping, and body throws are.

The thick silk belt worn by sumo wrestlers is called a *mawashi*. It is wound in a prescribed way to protect the wrestler's genitals as well as to provide a handhold for the contestants.

Like sumo wrestling and *taiko* drumming, traditional Japanese martial arts such as judo and kendo are a way of life in addition to being training in a particular skill. Some of the moves used by judo practitioners are derived from sumo throws and grappling maneuvers. Unlike sumo, where girth is an advantage, judo emphasizes flexibility and the efficient use of balance, leverage, and skill. Derived from jujutsu, a form of military exercise practiced by samurai usually without weapons, judo today is practiced for physical and mental conditioning, to develop self-confidence and to provide effective self-defense.

Kabuki is a Japanese form of theater incorporating elements and storylines from earlier Noh dramas and *Kyogen* plays, *Bunraku* puppet performances, and contemporary scandals in spectacles for the eyes and ears. Although the first performers were women, men took over all the roles in 1629. Styles of costuming and acting have been formalized over the centuries, culminating in a Kabuki actor's controlled and dancer-like performance today.

Kyozo Nakamura, an onnagata from the Grand Kabuki Troupe in Tokyo, performed at the Sakura Matsuri in 2001. An onnagata, an actor who specializes in female roles in the all-male Kabuki theater, wears a wig, make up, and a many-layered kimono in addition to using feminized movements and speech.

Judo, known as "the gentle way," has been an Olympic sport since 1964 and is derived from the ancient martial art of jujutsu. People of both sexes and all ages practice judo today as a sport, a discipline, and a way of life which emphasizes technique over stamina.

69

Children playing under the cherry blossoms are featured on sections of a low folding screen that might have framed a child's sleeping area in the 17th century. Their activities range from family blossom viewing to watching a cock fight, teasing a dog, a game of blind man's bluff, and playing with a ball and shuttlecock. Detail, Children at Play, Screen, *17th century, ink, color and gold on paper, 40.9 x 200.0 cm overall.*

For Japanese children, cherry blossom viewing time coincides with graduation and the beginning of a new school year. They might join their families for a party under the blooming trees, or they might participate in a school picnic. Children in the Washington area also picnic with their families, and attend some of the performances and events comprising the National Cherry Blossom Festival®. Children in both countries can enjoy Japanese folk tales anytime, one of which involves the blooming of a cherry tree.

The story is about a kind old man and his wife who lived in a village with their beloved dog, Shiro. Their mean next door neighbor and his wife hated the dog and would throw stones at him at every opportunity.

One day, Shiro was barking in the yard and the kind man realized the dog was showing him where to dig. So he dug, unearthing a pile of gold, which he took into his house.

The mean neighbor and his wife had been watch-

Japanese children long ago were included in picnics and other festivities under the cherry blossoms, just as they are today. The happy child shown here, dancing with her fan, perhaps reminds the inro's original owner of carefree hanami *picnics in her own childhood.*

70

American girls of different ages and backgrounds from the Shizumi Kodomo Dance Troupe wear kimonos and perform a traditional Japanese dance during opening ceremonies of the National Cherry Blossom Festival® in 2002.

ing secretly, and they wanted gold for themselves. The next day he asked to borrow the dog, and the kind man agreed. The mean man took Shiro to the field, watched where he started to dig, then began digging for himself. All he found was smelly rubbish. Outraged, he hit the dog with his shovel and killed him.

When the kind man learned what had happened, he was grief-stricken. He buried the dog's body in his own field under a pine tree. When it grew too big, he and his wife decided to cut it down to create a mortar to make rice cakes in memory of their dog. To their amazement the rice cakes made with the mortar were filled with gold, and once again the neighbor and his wife were overcome with jealousy.

The mean man asked to borrow the mortar to make rice cakes himself. When he tried, his were filled with stones. Angry and frustrated, he burned the mortar, leaving only a pile of ashes. The kind man took back the ashes to keep as a memento of Shiro. He scattered them upon a withered cherry tree which immediately began to blossom.

Everyone was astonished and even the prince heard about it. He asked the kind man to come to the castle to spread the ashes on his own favorite cherry tree that had died. The kind man obliged, scattering the ashes gently on the barren limbs, and the tree burst into spectacular bloom. The prince rewarded him with gold and a title.

The mean neighbor, now furious beyond bearing, offered to spread ashes on another dead tree and the prince accepted. The mean man tossed fistful after fistful of ash on the tree without result, except to have ash blown into the prince's eyes. Irritated and irate, the prince had the mean man jailed, while the kind man lived happily and richly ever after.

71

Japanese traditions and culture are showcased throughout the National Cherry Blossom Festival® in addition to the performances and demonstrations highlighted during the *Sakura Matsuri*. Music especially plays an important role throughout the Festival, contributing to the Japanese quality of many events and occasions. Typical Japanese instruments are played, such as the *koto*, the *shamisen*, and the bamboo flute.

Brought from China around the 7th century, C.E., the *koto* is similar to a zither and has thirteen strings. It is about six feet long, and made of paulownia wood. The strings are tuned by moving inverted Y-shaped bridges and are played by being plucked.

The three strings of the *shamisen*, a type of lute that resembles a banjo, are also plucked. Also imported from China, it has been popular since the beginning of the Edo Period and today *shamisen* music

The Opening Ceremony of the 2003 Cherry Blossom Festival featured a performance by the late Mannojo Nomura. Born into a Japanese theatrical family, famous for their association with Kyogen or classic comic theater emphasizing zany dialogue, Nomura's award-winning Dai Dengaku was performed at the National Cherry Blossom Festival® in the same year.

Some say that blind professional musicians were the only koto players until the late 17th century when cultivated Japanese, especially women and geishas, learned the skill. Washington Toho Koto Society players performed at the 2004 Lantern Lighting Ceremony.

accompanies many traditional theatrical performances, folk songs and dances.

The bamboo flute, called a *shakuhachi*, is played by blowing into one end of the tube, similar to playing a clarinet. It is about 1.8 feet long, the source of its name: *shaku* means about one foot and *hachi* means eight. Made from the lowest section of bamboo, the *shakuhachi* is known for its unique sound, combining

Origami cranes appear to float in the atrium of the National Building Museum during its Festival of Origami Architecture. Participants help create an origami city and pop-up buildings in addition to learning traditional paper-folding forms.

mellow and plaintive tones.

Origami, the well-known Japanese craft of paper-folding, is prominently featured among the Festival's events, including demonstrations at the *Sakura Matsuri* and one of the National Building Museum's events honoring the Festival. White origami cranes seem to fly through the air of the Museum's spectacular Great Hall, and participating families learn to make origami animals and other folded paper con-

structions. It is said that if you fold 1,000 cranes in a year, you will enjoy a lifetime of good luck. Other events celebrating Japanese culture include Japanese film marathons, and art and textile exhibitions.

Since 1994, the National Cherry Blossom Festival® has sponsored the Goodwill Ambassadors program. Goodwill Ambassadors serve as spokespeople for the Festival and are present at most events during the Festival. They also visit local schools and youth groups to broaden awareness and encourage greater understanding of Japan.

Goodwill Ambassadors are typically young men and women who are American students of Japanese language and culture, chosen by Festival committee members based on their educational and professional achievements, their understanding of the Japanese language, and their interest in promoting cultural exchange between the United States and Japan.

Washington area school children learn about the Japanese art of calligraphy by trying it themselves, displaying distinctive styles even as beginners. The pink-jacketed Goodwill Ambassadors bring their knowledge of Japanese language and culture into the wider community as just one aspect of their participation in the Festival.

Visitors to the National Cherry Blossom Festival® find fans used in many of the Festival performances, carried by Parade participants, and available for sale as souvenirs at the *Sakura Matsuri*, just as they would be found in Japan.

The first fans probably were large, stiff leaves waved to create cooling breezes or held above to provide protection from the sun or rain. Man-made fans were first produced by the Chinese and were used in Japan by the 8th century, C.E. Still used today, the flat round or paddle-shaped fans are called *uchiwa*.

The Japanese themselves take credit for inventing the folding fan, called *ogi*, and there are two myths about its origins. One legend says that its inventor was inspired by seeing the wings of a bat fold and unfold, and he glued paper to sticks to emulate them.

Shizumi Shigeto Manale performs with a large fan or ogi at a National Cherry Blossom Festival® event. Although her garment could suit modern dancers from any number of cultures, her use of the large fan is typical of Noh plays.

Twenty-six fans are painted directly on a 17th-century screen, giving the illusion that they are mounted individually. Scattered to suggest that they are floating through the air or on water, the fans depict natural beauty, famous sites and textile patterns for kimonos. With few ribs, all are of the style typically used by men. Decorated Fans, Edo period (1615–1868), Screen, color, ink and gold on paper,148 x 336 cm.

Cherry blossoms hand-painted on silk with a silvered paper edge form the fan supported by flat pierced-wood struts. The style of this 20th-century fan is reminiscent of hiogi *fans used by ladies of the Japanese Imperial Court until 1868.*

Fans remain closely associated with Japanese style and customs, and still are used today. The 1991 program cover designed by Wayne Fisher for the National Cherry Blossom Festival® shows the group of open fan-shaped motifs used as the visual theme for the Festival that year.

Another legend is that the widow of Atsumori, a Heian warrior whose death in battle at a young age is the subject of a Noh play, became a nun in her grief. She cured the abbot of the Mieido temple in Kyoto of a fever by fanning him with pleated paper which the monks copied.

Fans were and are used by men and women throughout Japan, and special forms evolved for particular uses. A ceremonial fan evolved for use in the Imperial Court, for example. Called a *hiogi*, it has thirty or more wooden slats and is decorated with prescribed images and styles. War fans were made of iron and used as signal devices in battle. Other fans serve as trays for food in the tea ceremony and props for Noh and Kabuki performances.

75

Many of the performing arts associated with *matsuri* in Japan are featured during the National Cherry Blossom Festival® each year. The Japanese and American amateur and professional groups who come to Washington to perform ancient songs, dances and plays lend an air of authenticity to the Festival, and connect it to its Japanese roots.

Performances of folk art forms and more refined traditions such as Noh plays remind their audiences of the deep spiritual roots of a *matsuri*. Intended to refresh and renew a community's connection with the divine, *matsuri* in Japan are exuberant celebrations with a spiritual dimension.

Many of the dances and performances at *matsuri* are based on ancient Shinto sacred dances and Buddhist plays. Some of the dances are simply joyful

Performances of Noh plays are often offered at matsuris in Japan. This woodblock print depicts a Noh play typically performed in the spring, called "Arashiyama," which refers to deities in the foothills northwest of Kyoto, an area known for its picturesque cherry trees and maples. Tsukioka Kogyo (1869–1927), Pictures of Noh Play: Arashiyama, *1902, Woodblock print, 228.6 x 331.79 mm.*

Dancers in 2003 in front of the Freer Gallery of Art perform a
Dai Dengaku, *a traditional Shinto dance invoking the spirit's blessing for a bountiful rice harvest. They carry a* kasa, *a form of umbrella that spreads the spirit's good will amongst the crowd when it is spun and shaken.*

while others are intended to drive away evil spirits. Still others refer to the rice-growing cycle. These folk traditions evolved over time into parts of the more formal Japanese theatrical performances such as Noh plays.

Many Noh plays in turn draw heavily on *The Tales of Heike*, the epic story of the war between two powerful warrior clans, culminating in the defeat of the Taira clan or Heike by the Minamoto clan in 1185. Like all great sagas, it includes heroes and villains, lovers and soldiers, brilliant strategies and unlucky twists of fate. The theme of the transitory and ephemeral quality of life closely associated with the cherry blossoms runs through the Noh plays, echoing their Bushido and Buddhist contexts.

Shizumi Shigeto Manale extends boughs of cherry blossoms in a performance during the National Cherry Blossom Festival® opening ceremonies, which highlight the friendship between the U.S. and Japan, the beauty and transitory nature of life as exemplified by the cherry blossoms, and the building of community the Festival engenders, just as matsuris *do in Japan.*

77

For nearly forty years, the Smithsonian Kite Festival has been a signature sign of spring in the Nation's Capital. It features kite-making and kite-flying competitions as well as a traditional rokkaku kite battle. In Japan, carp-shaped windsocks or streamers are flown on May 5, Children's Day.

Held for over thirty years, the Cherry Blossom 10-Miler is part of the Professional Road Running Organization (PRRO) circuit. World champions compete for more than $30,000 in prize money. Fun runs for adults and children are held also.

A competition is held each year to determine the winning design to be used for the National Cherry Blossom Festival® program cover, poster, commemorative t-shirt and other promotional materials and merchandise. The winner in 2004 was Jerry Arnold, an artist from Street, Maryland.

The National Cherry Blossom Festival® encompasses a myriad of other events beyond those that are primarily Japanese. The annual Smithsonian Kite Festival is held in conjunction with the Festival and features kite-flying competitions, special demonstrations, and kite-making activities.

Sports activities and events offer opportunities for spectators and competitors alike to enjoy the Festival. Typical of the events held during the Festival are: the Cherry Blossom 10-Mile Race with world-class runners among a field of 6,000; the National Cherry Blossom Festival® Golf Classic; the Cherry Blossom Lacrosse Tournament; and the George Washington Crew Classic.

Cherry trees are planted throughout the city, there is a Blessing of the Fleet at the U.S. Navy Memorial, and concerts are held in many different locations. Entertainments and galas are offered in a spectrum from casual to formal and from free to exclusive, some requiring a reservation and charging a fee.

Emphasizing the "festive" in festival, the National Cherry Blossom Festival® includes in its celebration a fireworks show, lighting up the night skies above the Tidal Basin and Potomac Park with a bright and colorful display as eye-catching and inspiring as the cherry blossoms themselves.

Fireworks light up the sky during the National Cherry Blossom Festival®. Appreciated for the gardens of light they create in the night sky, fireworks are an apt tribute to the cherry trees whose blossoms signal the end of bleak winter and the arrival of spring.

Cherry Blossoms Today
In Washington and Around the World

The Jefferson Memorial is now a favorite of visitors and Washington residents, though local society matrons protested its planned location in 1938 because in their view it would displace too many cherry trees.

Japanese Cherry Trees in Washington

The Japanese cherry trees in full bloom around the Tidal Basin are one of the landmark sights of Washington, D.C., on a par with the Washington Monument and the White House as a signature image of the Nation's Capital. The breathtaking beauty of the cherry blossoms is brief, lasting less than two weeks in total and at their peak for only a few days.

The trees are said to reach Peak Bloom when seventy percent of the single, white blossoms of the Yoshino cherry trees (*Prunus x yedoensis*) around the Tidal Basin are open, typically on April 4. The weather greatly affects their development, and unseasonably warm or cool temperatures can advance or delay the Peak Bloom significantly. The Yoshino cherry trees have reached their peak as early as March 15 in 1990, and as late as April 18 in 1958.

The Yoshino trees' buds are watched closely by National Park Service Horticulturists beginning in mid-winter, when they look for a green color to emerge in the buds. About three weeks prior to full bloom, florets are visible and regular progress reports are posted on the National Park Service web site, and covered by local news media who keep close tabs on the buds' growth as Peak Bloom nears and anticipation grows.

Extended florets indicate that roughly two weeks remain before Peak Bloom, and about six to ten days in advance, peduncle elongation is evident. Peduncle elongation refers to the lengthening of each flower's stalk that precedes its blooming. If temperatures drop into the mid- to low-20s or there is a heavy frost, parts of the blossoms may be damaged and there may be lighter bloom and seed set that season. The trees themselves, however, will survive undamaged.

In the four to six days prior to Peak Bloom, the Yoshino trees' buds become puffy and white, with an about-to-burst quality. Finally, they unfurl their delicate pink petals into the long-awaited blossoms and the Blooming Period begins. Lasting about two weeks, the Blooming Period encompasses the best time for people to throng to the Tidal Basin, Potomac Park, and the Washington Monument grounds to celebrate the end of winter, the promise of spring, and the enduring benefits of the great friendship between Japan and America.

Buds and blossoms on a Yoshino cherry tree show the different stages of bud development, from closed to peduncle elongation to puffy white to fully open. All the stages of bud development typically occur simultaneously on one tree, which is why the Blooming Period lasts about two weeks.

Tree Locator Map

Yoshino Cherry	*Prunus x yedoensis*	single, white flowers
Kwanzan Cherry	*Prunus serrulata 'Kwanzan'*	double, white flowers
Akebono Cherry	*Prunus x yedoensis 'Akebono'*	single, pale pink flowers
Takesimensis Cherry	*Prunus takesimensis*	single or double, white flowers
Usuzumi Cherry	*Prunus spachiana f. ascendens*	single, white-grey flowers
Weeping Japanese Cherry	*Prunus subhirtella var. pendula*	single or double, white to dark pink flowers
Autumn Flowering Cherry	*Prunus subhirtella var. autumnalis*	single or double, white to dark pink flowers
Sargent Cherry	*Prunus sargentii*	single, deep pink flowers
Fugenzo Cherry	*Prunus serrulata 'Fugenzo'*	double, rose pink flowers
Afterglow Cherry	*Prunus x yedoensis 'Afterglow'*	single, pink flowers
Shirofugen Cherry	*Prunus serrulata 'Shirofugen'*	double, white flowers
Okame Cherry	*Prunus x okame*	single or double, pink flowers

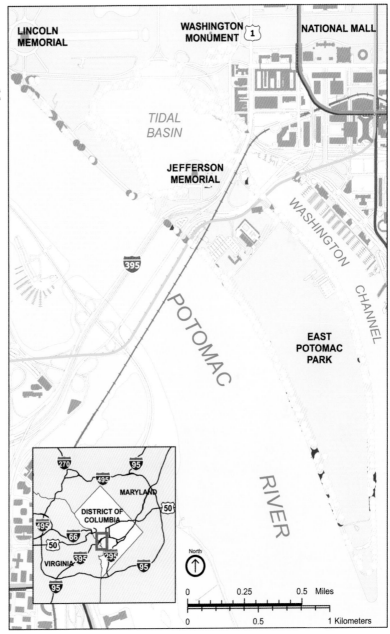

To ensure the trees' ongoing survival, the National Capital Region Cherry Tree Replacement Fund has been established. Managed by the National Park Foundation, the Cherry Tree Replacement Fund is an endowment fund where principal is invested and only interest earned is spent. It supports the care and maintenance of the famous trees in perpetuity, supplementing Congressional allocations and providing for emergencies such as floods and other natural or man-made disasters. Participating in the Cherry Tree Replacement Fund is a way for public-spirited organizations and private citizens to work together to continue the international goodwill and understanding signified by the original gift of the trees in 1912, and to maintain and enhance the trees' world-renowned beauty.

Japanese flowering cherry trees belong to the enormous family of woody and non-woody, ornamental and non-ornamental plants called *Rosaceae*, which includes among other genera, roses, apples, strawberries, brambles, almonds, and peaches. In fact, flowering cherry trees thrive in the same areas peaches do, with peach trees ranging a bit further south, and flowering cherries extending slightly further north beyond their common area. One of the largest concentrations of Yoshino cherry trees in the United States can be found in Macon, Georgia, where over 275,000 of the trees are planted throughout the city. A cherry blossom festival is held there every March, a highlight of spring in the Peach State.

More than 300 different varieties of Japanese ornamental cherry trees are known today, a result of the ease with which the trees can be propagated and adapted. They even transform themselves, with different colored blossoms sometimes occurring on a single tree. The trees vary according to shape and size,

This is a rare example of both white and deep pink blossoms found on one tree in Japan. They show the natural spectrum that horticulturists and geneticists work with, enhancing existing varieties and developing new ones. There are yellow and green cherry blossoms as well.

The almond-like scent of the Yoshino cherry trees is subtle and serves as a reminder that the trees belong in the huge Rosaceae family, which includes peaches, almonds, and apples in addition to roses and fruit-bearing cherry trees among many others.

color of bark, foliage patterns and "hairiness" of leaves, and type and timing of blooms.

Japanese cherry tree blossoms are categorized by color, size, number of petals, and other botanical attributes. The blooms can be pure white to deep

A bee in the midst of cherry blossoms demonstrates the role bees play in pollinating the cherry trees, bringing together the plant's male and female gametes or reproductive cells. The bees choose blossoms by color and patterns visible only to them, called nectar guides.

pink, and some are yellow to green. Blooms are referred to as "single" when there is one layer of five-notched petals, the image most frequently seen in artwork, on textiles and on metalwork. "Double" blooms indicate two or more layers of petals, with around thirty petals on a single bloom.

Different varieties flower at different times though each variety blooms simultaneously, and the blooming of all varieties is affected by the weather. The flowers can develop rapidly if there is an unusually warm period, and a cold snap can hold them at the bud stage for several days.

In some varieties, such as the Yoshino and Akebono trees planted around Washington's Tidal Basin, the flowers emerge before the leaves, creating the cloud-like effect their massed use is famous for. In other varieties, the flowers and the foliage open at about the same time, also lovely though perhaps with more dramatic rather than ethereal results.

Like all species in the genus *prunus*, Japanese cherry trees carry both male and female sex functions in their flowers, and they bear tiny fruit which birds devour, though humans would find them too small and bitter to be appealing. Other varieties, whose continuity depends on artificial propagation only, tend not to bear fruit.

Eliza Scidmore, one of the early proponents of bringing ornamental cherry trees to Washington, told a story about one of her many unsuccessful attempts to convince a new Superintendent of Public Buildings and Grounds to plant the trees in Potomac Park. In response to her suggestion, the man expressed wariness, reluctant to incur the police protection needed to prevent boys from climbing the trees and stealing the cherries. She countered that the trees only bore blossoms, not cherries. He remained unconvinced, saying "What good is that sort of a cherry tree?"

A sensational double cherry blossom from an unnamed selection, with too many delicate petals to count, is an example of one of the attributes that scientists strive to preserve in future varieties. Japanese cherry trees are notorious for their diversity, which led to the wide spectrum of cultivars available.

85

The Yoshino cherry, known as Somei-Yoshino in Japan and scientifically as *Prunus x yedoensis*, is not the same as the wild cherry trees found in the mountainous Yoshino district of Japan. The Yoshino cherry trees planted around the Tidal Basin were cultivated in the Imperial Botanic Garden in Tokyo, and have been recognized as a specific cultivar since 1872.

Early bloomers, Yoshino cherry trees usually grow to a height and spread of 30 feet with upright, spreading branches under a rounded top and smooth, grey bark. They are hardy in USDA zones 6-8. Their light pink buds open well before their foliage, and the faintly almond-scented flowers fade from pale pink to white. The trees' fruit is small, round and shiny black, and quickly eaten by birds.

The Akebono cherry tree, known as Daybreak (*Prunus x yedoensis* 'Akebono'), was named by W.B. Clarke of San Jose, California, in 1920. It is similarly shaped and only slightly smaller than a Yoshino, and its blossoms are pinker. In Washington, D.C., about 2700 Yoshino cherry trees surround the Tidal Basin, with more than 100 Akebono cherry trees interspersed among them. Akebono trees also are massed along the banks of the Willamette River in Portland, Oregon.

Two Afterglow cherry trees (*Prunus x yedoensis* 'Afterglow'), also closely related to Yoshino cherry trees, can be found in Potomac Park. The blooms are pinker than the Akebono blossoms when they open and they do not fade to white Like the Akebono cherry trees. Afterglow cherry trees reach a height and spread of twenty-five feet, making them about five feet smaller in both dimensions than Yoshinos. All three share an overall upright, spreading shape.

Only about 125 Yoshino cherry trees remain from the original gift of the trees in 1912. The trees encircling the Tidal Basin have about a fifty-year life span because of the high number of visitors who climb the trees, pluck their blossoms, and walk on the grass close to their trunks. Soil compaction is the

Akebono cherry trees are similar in size and shape to Yoshino cherry trees, and their distinctly pink blossoms also bloom before their foliage leafs out. Akebono cherry trees are intermingled among the Yoshinos around the Tidal Basin in Washington, D.C.

Located in northeast Washington, D.C., the National Arboretum has spectacular trees worth visiting. This large, old Yoshino cherry tree, Prunus x yedoensis, *can be found just beyond the edge of the National Herb Garden near the headquarters building.*

Left: Yoshino cherry trees around the Tidal Basin often sprout flowers from their trunks and branches. The Yoshino's gray bark is distinctive, and many of the trees' trunks seem to twist with age.

Right: The Yoshino cherry trees along the Tidal Basin's rim frame a view of the Washington Monument memorably when their foliage takes on striking autumnal hues.

greatest problem for the trees, forcing their roots to grow too close to the earth's surface to get the air they need. In less stressful environments, the trees can live for over one hundred years and in some cases in Japan are believed to have been alive for over 1000 years.

An ancient Japanese legend explains how some trees bear pink blossoms instead of white. In feudal times, a beautiful maiden named Masa lived with her father, Baisen, an old man and leader of rebels who planned to overthrow the Shogun and his family. Two rival knights, Kurondo and Makito, fell desperately in love with Masa but one, Kurondo, was a scoundrel and Masa spurned him. Kurondo learned of Baisen's association with the rebels and forced the old man at sword point to agree to betray Makito. Masa was to entice Makito to join her at their favorite meeting place under a cherry tree in full bloom, ply him with sake until he was drunk and an easy victim for Kurondo. To save her lover from death, Masa disguised herself as Makito, drank heavily of the rice wine, and lay under the tree. The deceit worked and Kurondo slew her when he came to the tree, believing he had killed Makito. The next spring, the cherry tree which had only borne white flowers before, covered itself with blossoms of deep pink, stained with the blood of the brave maiden.

87

The Kwanzan cherry trees in Potomac Park are identified by their profuse blossoms of clear pink. A cherry tree's "double" blossoms refers to any number of petals beyond a "single" layer of five, and a Kwanzan blossom may have about thirty petals.

Kwanzan cherry trees, named for a Japanese mountain, are found primarily in East Potomac Park. Also called Kanzan, Sekizan or Seki-yama, Kwanzan trees or *Prunus serrulata* 'Kwanzan' are popular for their double pink flowers with around thirty petals which hang in heavy clusters composed of three to five blossoms. Taller than Yoshino trees, they grow to about 30 feet in a vase shape, have a dark reddish-brown bark, and are hardy in USDA zones 5-8. They bloom two weeks after the Yoshino trees, and at about the same time as the rose-pink Fugenzo (*Prunus serrulata* 'Fugenzo') and white-flowered Shiro-fugen (*Prunus serrulata* 'Shirofugen'). Kwanzan trees are best viewed from below to enjoy the beauty of their hanging flower clusters. There are 481 Kwanzan cherry trees in Potomac Park, along with fourteen Fugenzo trees and one Shirofugen tree.

The Kwanzan, Shiro-fugen (White Goddess) and Fugenzo (Goddess on a White Elephant) are all varieties of oriental cherry trees in the species *Prunus serrulata*. Another variety in the same species is called Mikuruma Gaeshi, or "The Royal Carriage Returns." Mikuruma Gaeshi trees were one of the types of trees sent to Washington in 1912 but are no longer found in Potomac Park. The tradition behind their intriguing name is that an early emperor, enjoying a spring drive in the country, was so taken with the beauty of a particular cherry tree in full flower that he ordered his carriage to return to the spot so he could enjoy the sight once again. The specific tree no longer exists, but it is said to be the forebear of all the trees of this variety.

Japanese weeping or Higan cherry trees belong to the species *Prunus subhirtella*, which blooms about one week before the Yoshinos. "Higan" means equinox in Japanese, reflecting the tendency of these trees to bloom at the time of the spring equinox. Some varieties, called Autumn Flowering Cherry, bloom sporadically during warm periods in the fall, often coinciding with the fall equinox, and fully flower in the spring.

Higan cherry trees vary widely in shape, and in form and color of the flowers. The bark is usually gray, and the flowers typically bloom before the foliage emerges, creating a mass effect as impressive as that of the Yoshino cherry trees. They are hardy in USDA zones 5-8. More than ninety weeping Japanese cherry trees or *Prunus subhirtella* var. pendula are found in Potomac Park, as well as about twenty Autumn Flowering cherry trees (*Prunus subhirtella* var. autumnalis) whose display of blossoms during "Indian summers" in the fall startle and delight Washington's residents and visitors.

Another variety found in numbers in Potomac Park is Takesimensis (*Prunus takesimensis*). 190 are being tested for hardiness in Washington's humid climate because the species is a native of wet locations in Korea. Takesimensis cherry trees can reach forty feet, and bear white flowers in large clusters.

A weeping cherry tree, Prunus subhirtella pendula, *with its distinctive cascade of pink flowers, blooms exuberantly in the midst of tulips at Filoli Gardens, Woodside, California.*

Usuzumi cherry trees (*Prunus spachiana* f. ascendens) are distinctive because of their pedigree and unusual flowers. The trees were grown from cuttings from the "Usuzumi-No-Sakura" tree, declared a National Treasure in 1922 and said to be the largest in Japan. Legend says that the 26th Emperor Keitai Tenno planted the tree 1500 years ago to commemorate the eighteen years he lived happily in Neo Mura Village in Gifu Prefecture where the tree is found. Usuzumi cherry trees reach a height of forty feet with gray bark and single flowers which are pink-tinged at first, then turn white and finally grey before falling. The fifty Usuzumi trees in Potomac Park were planted in 1999 as a gift to Washington, D.C., from the people of Neo Mura Village, with the support of a number of sponsors. Five are located to the west of

the Jefferson Memorial, and the others are grouped between the Potomac River and Ohio Drive in the northwest section of West Potomac Park.

More than twenty specimens of one of the largest cherry trees, the Sargent cherry (*Prunus sargentii*) can also be found in Potomac Park. Hardy in USDA zones 4-7, growing to a height of sixty feet, with smooth dark brown bark, its single flowers are clear pink. The foliage turns brilliant shades of scarlet and crimson in the autumn.

Potomac Park's lone Okame cherry tree (*Prunus incam* 'okame') is the earliest flowering cherry. A hybrid between a Fuji cherry tree (*Prunus incisa*) and a Taiwan cherry tree (*Prunus campanulata*) an Okame tree has an oval shape, a height of twenty-five feet and spread of twenty feet, with brightly colored buds and flowers.

The Kwanzan cherry tree has reddish-green foliage that emerges while the tree is blooming and turns an attractive bronze-orange color in the fall. The Kwanzan trees flower ten to fourteen days after the Yoshinos. KANZAN, Prunus lannesiana *'Sekiyama.'*

89

Care and Propagation

Ornamental cherry trees are propagated either by rooted cuttings or by budding or grafting. To propagate by rooting, experts take cuttings of soft wood from the spring growth, treat it with a rooting hormone, then put it in soil-less media under mist on a heated bench. Some varieties like 'Dream Catcher' root easily while others, like 'First Lady,' require propagation by budding or grafting.

Budding or grafting means that a bud or stick or scion of the variety to be propagated is carefully spliced onto rootstock of a different type of tree, allowing the cultivar to benefit from the first tree's root system. Both propagation techniques demand practice and skill, followed by proper pruning to train the cherry trees to grow into desirable shapes. Some

The National Park Service Cherry Tree Maintenance Crew of certified arborists is entrusted to maintain the Japanese cherry trees in Potomac Park. They prune the trees twice each year: first, beginning in January through blooming, to maintain the trees' shape and remove dead limbs, then through the summer to remove suckers.

Scientists at the National Arboretum pollinate cherry blossoms by hand using a tiny paint brush to fertilize a flower. They mix the male and female gametes of different varieties, seeking to improve attributes of the trees such as flowering, bark attractiveness, hardiness, and disease and pest resistance.

cherry trees also can be grown from seed, although the seedlings will differ from the parent trees, risking a change in the variety's attributes, so vegetative propagation by rooting or budding or grafting is preferred.

Japanese cherry trees prefer full sun and well-drained soil. Plant new trees in the fall, with mulch out to the ends of their branches. They are subject to borers, and some varieties are susceptible to diseases. Trees that are chosen to suit their environment and are well-cared for, however, are likely to thrive.

The first three to six years are the most important in the development of a healthy and attractive ornamental cherry tree. To create a strong scaffold branch structure and pleasing shape, multiple leaders need to be encouraged which means selecting permanent lateral branches spaced six to twelve inches apart all around the tree. The best size for leaders is one half or less the diameter of the tree's trunk at the point of attachment.

The Cherry Tree Maintenance Crew of professional arborists takes care of the cherry trees in Potomac Park. Pruning is the most important task they perform, training young trees with a modified leader system, creating the scaffold branching form they maintain in the older trees. In addition to watering, fertilizing, treating wounds, and controlling pests and diseases, the Tree Crew works to mitigate the effects of soil compaction around the trees due to the large numbers of visitors. All of the Japanese cherry trees in Potomac Park are mapped and inventoried, and on average, two to four percent of the trees are lost each year to old age or diseases.

The trees around the Tidal Basin face another threat: beavers. In 1999 several cherry trees were felled by the aquatic rodents endemic to the Potomac River area. Those particular beavers were trapped and transported elsewhere, but evidence of their work can be found today, especially on Roosevelt Island. It's not a matter of "if" the beavers will return, but "when."

Prunus 'First Lady' is the newest variety of cherry tree to be introduced by the National Arboretum. Early bloomers with a tall, columnar shape, their semi-pendulous single blossoms are the darkest pink.

The U.S. National Arboretum

Geneticist Dr. Margaret Pooler and her colleagues at the U.S. National Arboretum are developing new varieties of ornamental cherry trees. They aim to create a flowering cherry tree that will thrive in the widest range of climates and conditions in the U.S., be disease and pest resistant, and bloom beautifully, presenting an attractive shape and bark when leafless.

The Arboretum has introduced two new varieties in recent years: 'Dream Catcher' (*Prunus* 'Dream Catcher') and 'First Lady' (*Prunus* 'First Lady'). Both are derived from the Okame cherry tree (*Prunus x incam* 'Okame'). 'First Lady,' introduced in 2003, is a tall, columnar-shaped tree which will reach a height of twenty-five feet and a spread of fourteen feet. It is an early bloomer and its semi-pendulous single flowers are the darkest pink.

'Dream Catcher' is the other new tree, introduced in 1999. It is tall, of an oval shape and with a height similar to the 'First Lady' cherry tree. It is early blooming, with medium pink, single blossoms and colorful fall foliage, and is valued especially for its dark green pest-tolerant summer foliage.

It takes at least twenty years to develop a new tree from a seed or propagated seedling before it is ready to distribute to the public. In addition to flowering cherries (*Prunus*), the Arboretum geneticists are working to develop new varieties of red buds (*Cercis*) and crape myrtles (*Lagerstroemia*), and other woody ornamental plants.

Dr. Pooler and her colleagues also have worked on preserving older varieties of trees. In 1997, cuttings were taken from Yoshino cherry trees documented to be from the 1912 shipment from Japan and 500 saplings were successfully grown. Some of the saplings will be used in replacement plantings to preserve the genetic heritage of the cherry trees around the Tidal Basin, and others will be planted elsewhere to maintain a healthy mix of different varieties.

91

Cherry Trees in Japan

Today, just as they have for more than a thousand years, people throughout Japan celebrate the blooming of the cherry trees with cherry blossom viewing parties or *hanami*. Cherry blossom festivals or *sakura matsuri* are held when the blooms are at their peak. Because of Japan's north-south orientation, the peak bloom arrives first in southern-most Okinawa as early as January and moves north, followed attentively by the media as the Cherry Front, arriving in Tokyo and Kyoto in early April and moving on to northern Hokkaido in May.

Early April is also the beginning of the new school year and many corporate fiscal years, and the *hanami* parties celebrate those new beginnings as well as the blossoms, which signal the coming of spring. Some employees spend their first day at new jobs staking out prime blossom-viewing spots with big blue tarps for their company's *hanami* party, usually a large picnic with food, drink and music.

Hanami also means the feeling of losing oneself in the clouds of blossoms, or focused on a single bloom. The 17th-century poet Basho captured its essence in the following haiku:

> *A cloud of flowers*
> *A bell rings*
> *At Ueno? Or Asakusa?*

As has been true for centuries, Japanese people today from all walks of life are moved deeply by the spectacular and brief bloom of the cherry trees, as are people wherever the trees grow. A poem by a 19th-century Japanese poetess expresses this exquisitely:

Blooming cherry trees are juxtaposed against a screen of pines in classic Japanese style behind a wall surrounding the famous Abbot's Garden at Ryoanji Temple in Kyoto. The garden's meaning remains elusive, interpreted by some to be islands in the sea or a tigress swimming with her cubs.

> *When the cherry blossoms bloomed*
> *They brought beauty to my heart.*
>
> Tatsu-Jo

A longer poem by Her Majesty The Empress of Japan also conveys the universal experience of awe in the beauty of the moment, and melancholy in its brevity.

> *People here and there,*
> *Lingering as if to share*
> *A moment of joy,*
> *Gazing where at the close of day*
> *The blossoms fall in town.*

Wherever the blossoms fall, they remind us to make the most of every day, of all of our talents and opportunities, that even the most ordinary can be transformed into something extraordinary, and that all things pass, vanishing into the mists of memory, remembered in our hearts.

Some of the well-known places to view cherry blossoms in Japan today are:

Tokyo: Ueno Park, Shinjaku Gyoen Park, Edo Castle Moat
Osaka: Osaka Mint, Osaka Castle
Kyoto: Philosopher's Trail, Maruyuma Park, Heian Shrine, Arashiyama
Nagoya: Nagoya Castle

Mount Fuji is the highest mountain in Japan and has been worshipped as a sacred mountain for eons. Climbing to its top is considered a pilgrimage by many Japanese. To the rest of the world, Mount Fuji is as closely identified with Japan itself as is the cherry blossom.

Selected Viewing Locations in the U.S. For Japanese Flowering Cherry Trees

Arnold Arboretum of Harvard University, Jamaica Plain, Massachusetts
Brooklyn Botanic Garden, Brooklyn, New York
Brookside Gardens, Silver Spring, Maryland
The Cornell Plantations, Ithaca, New York
Filoli Center, Woodside, California
The Holden Arboretum, Kirtland, Ohio
Huntington Library, Art Collections, and Botanical Gardens, San Marino, California
Longwood Gardens, Kennett Square, Pennsylvania
Missouri Botanical Garden, Saint Louis, Missouri
Morris Arboretum and Gardens of the University of Pennsylvania, Philadelphia, Pennsylvania
The Morton Arboretum, Lisle, Illinois
The New York Botanical Garden, Bronx, New York
The Botanic Garden of Smith College, Northampton, Massachusetts
San Francisco Botanical Gardens, San Francisco, California
Tyler Arboretum, Media, Pennsylvania
U.S. National Arboretum, Washington, D.C.
Washington Park Arboretum, Seattle, Washington

Plump buds open to reveal delicate petals throughout the two-week Blooming Period, giving Washingtonians and visitors ample opportunity to enjoy the evanescent beauty of the flowering cherry trees.

Selected Cherry Blossom Festivals Around the U.S.

Brooklyn, New York
Cupertino, California
Denver, Colorado
Honolulu, Hawaii
Macon, Georgia
Monterey Park, California
Pasadena, California
Philadelphia, Pennsylvania
San Francisco, California
Seattle, Washington

Other festivals celebrate fruit-bearing cherry trees, such as the National Cherry Festival, Traverse City, Michigan, held each July.

National Capital Region Cherry Tree Replacement Fund

In 2003, the National Park Service (NPS) established the National Capital Region Cherry Tree Replacement Fund to supplement the amount appropriated by Congress for the replacement and maintenance of the cherry trees. NPS works with partners such as the National Cherry Blossom Festival®, corporations, local businesses, civic organizations such as the Rotary Club of Washington, D.C., and individuals from the U.S., Japan, and other countries. The National Parks Foundation manages the donations as an endowment fund for the NPS, which plans to use the Fund to ensure the perpetual care and maintenance of the world-renowned cherry trees.

For more information, contact the NPS Partnership Office, 1100 Ohio Drive, S.W., Room 350, Washington, D.C. 20242 or visit www.nps.gov/cherry/cherryfund.html.

Akebono cherry trees display distinctive pink blossoms among the predominant Yoshino cherry trees around the Tidal Basin each spring.

The National Cherry Blossom Festival®

The National Cherry Blossom Festival® is Washington, D.C.'s signature spring event. It is a two-week city-wide celebration of international friendship and the gift of 3,000 cherry trees to the United States from Japan in 1912. Held annually, it begins the last week of March and continues through the first week of April coinciding, when Mother Nature cooperates, with the blooming of the cherry trees. The Festival features daily international and local cultural performances, sporting events, arts and crafts demonstrations, food events, tours, art exhibits, neighborhood tree plantings, and other special events. Highlights each year include the National Cherry Blossom Festival Parade® and the Japan-America Society of Washington, D.C.'s *Sakura Matsuri* – Japanese Street Festival. For more information, visit the web site at www.nationalcherryblossomfestival.org.

Performances of Japanese martial arts, music, and dance take place in many locations in Washington during the two-week-long Festival. The steps and promenade in front of the Jefferson Memorial are popular for observers as this taiko drumming demonstration shows.

95

Acknowledgements

The clouds of pink Japanese cherry blossoms in Washington, the international friendship they stand for and the Festival that honors them have inspired many, especially the wonderful people I encountered while doing research for this book. Their generosity of spirit was remarkable, and it was a privilege to meet and work with each of them.

The Board members and staff of the National Cherry Blossom Festival® (NCBF) went to great lengths to share information and images, and to make sure important aspects of the history of the trees and the Festival were clear. Jackie Wolfe, Past President and Chairman, was specially forthcoming and helpful from start to finish. Diana Mayhew, Executive Director, and Lillian Iversen, Program Assistant, were generous with their time, expertise and insights.

Laurel Lukaszewski, Vice Chair of the NCBF Board and Executive Director of the Japan-America Society of Washington, D.C., Barbara Ehrlich, Treasurer of the NCBF Board, and Paul MacLardy, Program Chair of the NCBF Board and owner of Arise Galleries, were all tremendously responsive, providing materials and guiding me to useful information. Marc Hitzig and Aki Watanuki of the Japan-America Society were helpful with *Sakura Matsuri* details, insights about modern Japanese language and life, and provided access to the Society's excellent library.

Members of the National Conference of State Societies (NCSS) were generous with their time and resources, reflecting the NCSS' long association with the Cherry Blossom Festival, especially Mark Rhoads, Past President, Paul Sweet, President, and Dee Shallenberger. Akiko Keene, NCSS liaison with the Japan Cherry Blossom Association, went to extraordinary lengths to provide information and obtain images.

Representatives of the National Park Service, National Capital Region, were helpful and knowledgeable, especially Robert A. De Feo, Glenn Eugster, Cathy Nelson, Terry J. Adams and Margie Ortiz. Similarly, Dr. Margaret Pooler of the National Arboretum was generous with her time and expertise.

Several museums and their staffs were sources for information as well as guidance regarding illustrative material. Ann Yonemura, of the Freer Gallery of Art and Arthur M. Sackler Gallery, was particularly helpful and encouraging as were her colleagues, Rebecca Barker and Cory Grace. Bruce Coats of Scripps College, Sandra Knudsen, of the Toledo Museum of Art, and Hiram Woodward of The Walters Art Museum all were similarly generous. Meher McArthur of the Pacific Asia Museum shared both her knowledge and her photographic skills. Nancy Korber of the Fairchild Tropical Garden was creative and persistent in her research assistance, with stunning results.

Ann Marie Moeller of Arise Galleries shared her deep knowledge and keen enthusiasm for all things Japanese, as did Kurt Kumagai, Marketing Director. Others whose research skills or information were helpful include Carolyn Crouch of Washington Walks, Mark Jenkins of the National Geographic Society, and Vicki Killian, an expert researcher. The staff at the Japan Information and Culture Center in Washington helped locate appropriate resources and contacts.

Those who were helpful in finding illustrations were: Peggy Appleman, DC Public Library; Nancy Buley, J. Frank Schmidt & Son, Company; Holly Reed and Mary E. Linné, National Archives and Records Administration; and Gail Rodgers Redmann, the Historical Society of Washington, D.C. Hiromi Nakaoji served as the intermediary with the Ozaki Memorial in Ise City, Japan, and with Miss Mieko Ishikawa, a botanical illustrator in Japan, specializing in flowering cherries and tropical plants in Borneo.

The Washington area photographers whose work is represented include: Steve Alterman, Marvin Ickow, Judy Rolfe (www.rolfephotography.com), John Swank (www.fwphotos.com), and Susan Soroko representing Folio Inc. (www.foliophoto.com). Expert and invaluable technical assistance was provided by Chuck Livingston, Eason Associates, and Etshiwot Nani Mulatu, ABC Imaging. Marvin Ickow and Natoy Putney, ABC Imaging, were fellow adventurers in exploring new technological possibilities.

The support of my family and friends was invaluable, especially Helen Bergman, Frances Stevenson, and Becky Eason and her colleagues at Eason Associates where temporary work space came with good-humored advice and collegiality.

Lastly, I am deeply grateful to Ib Bellew and Carole Kitchel of Bunker Hill Publishing for the opportunity, their vision and confidence, and to Louise Millar whose design adds zest and verve.

ANN MCCLELLAN

Professional and amateur photographers alike enjoy the challenge of capturing the beauty of the cherry blossoms and their dramatic setting around the Tidal Basin.

97

Notes on Sources

The publisher and author wish to thank those who have granted kind permission to reproduce images owned or produced by them, or to include poems or excerpts written by them on the pages indicated. Every effort has been made to trace the copyright of all sources and the publishers will be happy to redress any errors or omissions in future editions.

The translations of the following poems are from *The Moon in the Pines: Zen Haiku*, selected and translated by Jonathan Clements, published by Frances Lincoln Ltd., copyright © 2000, reproduced by permission of Frances Lincoln Ltd., 4 Torriano Avenue, London NW5 2RZ: Basho, pages 40, 45, 92; Issa, page 14; Tatsu-jo, page 92; Teishitsu, page 8.

The translation of the Motoöri poem on page 9 is taken from *Myths and Legends of Japan*, by F. Hadland Davis, London: George G. Harrap & Company, Ltd., 1912.

Ms. Aki Watanuki assisted with the translation of the "Sakura Song" on page 9.

The translation of the poem by Yoshiie on page 10 by Joshua Mostow is reproduced with his permission.

The poem attributed to Emperor Shomu on page 14 is from a handwritten note by David Fairchild, 1913/1914.

The anonymous haiku on page 16 is from Haiku for People, www.toyomasu.com.

The translation of the "Ancient Japanese Poem" on page 26 is from *Jinrikisha Days* by Eliza Scidmore, New York: Harper & Brothers, 1891. Other quotes from Ms. Scidmore are from her articles in *The Century Magazine, The Sunday Star,* and *The Washington Star,* as noted in the Bibliography.

The excerpt on page 41 from *The Japanese Cherry Trees in Washington, D.C.* by Maud Kay Sites, Baltimore: Norman T.A. Munder, 1935, is reproduced by permission of Special Collections, Enoch Pratt Free Library/Resource Center, Baltimore, Maryland.

The poem by Her Majesty the Empress of Japan on page 92 is included by permission of the Office of the Imperial Household, General Affairs Division, 1-1, Chiyoda, Chiyoda-ku, Tokyo, Japan.

Primary Sources Consulted

National Archives, Washington, D.C. and College Park, Maryland, Record Group 42: included correspondence, images, and other material related to the Office of Public Buildings and Grounds
Fairchild Tropical Gardens Special Collections: unpublished articles, notes, and correspondence of David and Marian Bell Fairchild
Washingtoniana Division, Washington, D.C., Public Library: *Washington Evening Star* photographs plus scrapbooks, ephemera, clippings

Picture Credits

The publisher and the author wish to thank the following for their kind permission to reproduce the images which appear on the pages noted. Every effort has been made to trace the copyright of all sources and the publishers will be happy to redress any errors or omissions in future editions.

Front cover: Kawase Hasui (1883-1957), *Washington Monument (Potomac Riverbank)*, Detail, Woodblock print, 39.0 x 26.0 cm. Arthur M. Sackler Gallery, Smithsonian Institution, Washington, D.C.: Gift of the Kruglak family in memory of Amy & Ted Kruglak, S1998.159

Back cover: artwork by Joan Lok, 2005 National Cherry Blossom Festival® Art Contest Winner.

Endpapers: Ando Hiroshige II (1826-1869), *Flower Paths: Procession of Women*, 1857, Woodblock print, 366.71 x 746.13mm. Scripps College, Claremont, California: 46.1.168

Title Page: *Prunus* 'Dream Catcher,' ©Keith Warren, J. Frank Schmidt & Son Co.

4: Terry J. Adams, National Park Service

5: Utagawa Hiroshige (1842?-1894), *Cherry Blossoms in Full Bloom along Sumida River, from The Most Beautiful Place in Tokyo*, Woodblock print triptych. Library of Congress, Prints and Photographs Division: Gift of Mrs. E. Crane Chadbourne, 606378-LC-USZC4-10934

6-7: Hishikawa Moronobu (1618-1694), *Viewing Cherry Blossoms at Ueno Park*, Ink, color and gold on paper, 165.6 H x 367.8 W cm. Freer Gallery of Art, Smithsonian Institution, Washington, D.C.: Gift of Charles Lang Freer, F1906.267

8: Utagawa Hiroshige (1797-1858), *Sunset at Koganei Bridge*, Woodblock print, 34.9 x 22.2 cm. The Art Institute of Chicago: Clarence Buckingham Collection, 1925.3413

9: Katsushika Hokusai (1760-1849), *Cherry Flowers at Yoshino*, 1836, Woodblock print, oban. The Art Institute of Chicago: Gift of Mr. and Mrs. Gaylord Donnelley, 1969.695

10: Sumiyoshi Hironao (1781-1828), *Minamoto no Yoshiie at Nakoso Barrier*, Hanging Scroll, Ink, color and gold on silk, 193.2 x 55.3 cm. Freer Gallery of Art, Smithsonian Institution, Washington, D.C.: Gift of Mr. Kenneth Keith, F1999.11

11 left: National Archives, Brady Collection, III B-2325

11 right: Ishikawa Komei, Carved elephant tusk vase, ca. 1880. The Walters Art Museum, Baltimore: 71.1080

12: Shunsui, Edo Period (1603-1868), Inro, Lacquer with black ground. Toledo Museum of Art: Gift of H.A. Fee, 1952.47

13 upper: Tosa Mitsuoki (1617-1691), *The Visit of Sochi and Kashiwagi to the New Palace*, from the *Tales of Genji*, Detail, Screen, Ink, color and gold on paper, 171.1 x 376.8 cm. Freer Gallery of Art, Smithsonian Institution, Washington, D.C.: Gift of Charles Lang Freer, F1904.118

13 lower: *Wind-screen and cherry tree*, Screen, Edo period (1615-1868), Color over gold on paper, 148.1 x 341.1 cm. Freer Gallery of Art, Smithsonian Institution, Washington, D.C.: Gift of Charles Lang Freer, 1897.3

14: Toyohara Chikanobu (1838-1912), *Snow, Moon, Flower-Edo; Flower of Ueno, Cherry Blossoms at Mt. Toei*, Ink on paper, 325.44 x 215.9mm. Scripps College, Claremont, California: 93.6.63

15 upper: Tosa Mitsuoki (1617-1691), *Flowering Cherry with Poem Slips*, c. 1675, One of a pair of six-fold screens, Ink, colors and gold on silk, 142.5 x 293.2 cm. The Art Institute of Chicago: Kate S. Buckingham Collection, 1977.156, Photography by Robert Hashimoto

15 lower: Gakutei Harunobu, 19th century, *Two Geishas Reading from a Book*, Hanging scroll, Color, gold and silver on silk, 56.6 x 87.0 cm. Freer Gallery of Art, Smithsonian Institution, Washington, D.C.: Gift of Charles Lang Freer, 1898.8

16: Ando Hiroshige (1797-1858), *Famous Places of the Eastern Capital*, c. 1832-1855, Woodblock print 33.97 x 75.57 cm. Scripps College, Claremont, California: 93.3.182

17 left: Hosoda Eishi (1756-1829), *Beauties of the Season - Spring*, early 19th century, Detail, Full color on silk, 175.6 x 49.8 cm. Freer Gallery of Art, Smithsonian Institution, Washington, D.C.: Purchase, F1957.7

17 right: Utagawa Toyokuni III, Woodblock print ca.1847-52, oban. Japan-America Society, Washington, D.C.

18: Artist unknown, *Festival at Yoshiwara*, Ink on paper, 33.81 x 46.83 cm. Scripps College, Claremont, California: 98.8.20

19 left: Utagawa Toyokuni III, 1852, Woodblock print, oban. Japan-America Society of Washington, D.C.

99

19 right: Utagawa Kunisada, (1786-1864), *The Actor Bando Mitsugoro III as the Maiden of Dojoji*, Woodblock print, 1816, 36.3 x 25.6 cm, oban. Arthur M. Sackler Gallery, Smithsonian Institution, Washington, D.C.: Lent by Anne Van Biema, LTS2004.1.130

20: Artist unknown, *Taisho Emperor and Empress*, Scripps College, Claremont, California: 93.8.1

21 upper: Kawashima Shigenobu (ca. 1722-1744), Handscroll, Ink, color and gold on paper, 33.0 x 829.0 cm. Freer Gallery of Art, Smithsonian Institution, Washington, D.C.: Purchase, 1975.27

21 lower: Ando Hiroshige II (1826-1869), *Flower Paths: Procession of Women*, 1857, Woodblock print, 366.71 x 746.13mm. Scripps College, Claremont, California: 46.1.168

22: James McNeill Whistler (1834-1903), *Caprice in Purple and Gold: The Golden Screen*, 1864, Oil on wood, 50.2 x 68.7 cm. Freer Gallery of Art, Smithsonian Institution, Washington, D.C.: Gift of Charles Lang Freer, 1904.75a

23 upper: Artist unknown, Edo Period 1603-1868, Inro, Lacquer, mother-of-pearl and gold-foil inlays. Toledo Museum of Art: Gift of H.A. Fee, 1948.155

23 lower: Toyohara Kunichika (1835-1900), *Tokyo Ueno Second Industrial Exhibition*, 1881, Woodblock print, oban triptych, 35.7 x 71.8 cm. Scripps College, Claremont, California: 2001.2.28

24-5: National Archives: RG 42-MS-148

26: Copyright Washington Post; reprinted by permission of the DC Public Library

27 left: Washington Historical Society/City Museum: CHS 2415

27 right: National Archives: RG-42, Potomac Park 52/313

28: Fairchild Tropical Botanic Garden Special Collections

29 left: National Archives: RG 16-G, Box 21-F, 25275C

29 right: YAEBENISHIDARE, *Prunus Pendula* "Plena-rosea" © Mieko Ishikawa

30 upper: Library of Congress, Prints and Photographs Division: 606376-LC-USZ62-25804

30 lower: National Archives: RG 42-WH 12-15

31: National Archives: RG 42-Potomac Park 52/313

32-34, 35 left: Fairchild Tropical Botanical Garden Special Collections

35 right: Copyright Washington Post; reprinted by permission of the DC Public Library

36: Copyright Washington Post; reprinted by permission of the DC Public Library

37 left: *Japanese Cherry Blossoms*, Detroit Publishing Company, glass transparency, 1900- 1915. Library of Congress, Prints and Photographs Division: Gift of State Historical Society of Colorado, 1949, 606379-LC-D418-73523

37 right: National Archives: RG 42-MS-145

38 left: Fairchild Tropical Botanic Garden Special Collections

38 right: Frances Benjamin Johnston (1864-1952), *Mills Thompson*, photographic print, ca. 1890-1910, Library of Congress, Prints & Photographs Division: 606376-LC-USZ62-47067

39 upper: Photographic print, 1909-1932. Library of Congress Prints & Photographs Division: National Photo Company Collection, 606938-LC-USZ62-96748

39 lower: Martha McMillan Roberts, *Cherry Blossom Festival*, negative nitrate, May 1941. Library of Congress Prints & Photographs Division: Office of War Information Photograph Collection, 607521- LC-USF34-014450-E

40: Postcard, B.S. Reynolds Company, Publisher; Judy Rolfe Collection

41 left: Ozawa Nankoku, (1844-?), *Owl in Moonlight*, Hanging scroll, Ink and color on silk with ivory jiku, 166 x 82.3 cm overall. Freer Gallery of Art, Smithsonian Institution, Washington, D.C.: Purchase from the Estate of Robert O. Muller, F2004.12

41 right: ©Sucha Snidvongs, National Cherry Blossom Festival®

42 left & right, 43 upper: Copyright Washington Post; reprinted by permission of the DC Public Library

43 lower: Terry J. Adams, National Park Service

44 left: © Marvin Ickow

44 right & 45 upper: Copyright Washington Post; reprinted by permission of the DC Public Library

45 lower: ©1934 Washington Post, reprinted with permission; Library of Congress, Prints & Photographs Division, Clifford Berryman Collection, acd 2a06434

46: © Steve Alterman

47 left: Terry J. Adams, National Park Service

47 right: Lyndon Baines Johnson Library and Museum; 34199-13

48-9: © Judy Rolfe

50, 51 left: Copyright Washington Post; reprinted by permission of the DC Public Library

51 right: The Historical Society of Washington, D.C./City Museum

52 & 53: Copyright Washington Post; reprinted by permission of the DC Public Library

54: ©Solomon Stoddard, National Cherry Blossom Festival®

55 left: Copyright Washington Post; reprinted by permission of the DC Public Library

55 right: Ronald Reagan Library, with thanks to National Conference of State Societies

56-7: ©Ron Engle, National Cherry Blossom Festival®

57 upper right: ©Ron Engle, National Cherry Blossom Festival® and ©2004 Sesame Workshop. "Sesame Street" and its logo are trademarks of Sesame Workshop. All rights reserved.

58, 59 upper two and lower left: ©Ron Engle, National Cherry Blossom Festival®

59 lower right: ©Stephen Schaffer, National Cherry Blossom Festival®

60: Ando Hiroshige (1797-1858), *The Fifty-three Stations of Tokaido, Miya (Station 42), Festival at Atsuta Shrine,* c. 1833-34, Woodblock print, 222.25 x 3406.08 mm. Scripps College, Claremont, California: 46.1.17

61 upper two: ©Ron Engle, National Cherry Blossom Festival®

61 lower right: Judy Rolfe, articles courtesy Arise Gallery

62, 63 upper: © Freer Gallery of Art and Arthur M. Sackler Gallery, Smithsonian Institution, Washington, D.C.

63 lower: Library of Congress, Prints & Photographs Division: National Photo Art Company, ca. 1902, 606376-LC-USZ62-75162

64 left: ©Ron Engle, National Cherry Blossom Festival®

64 right: ©Gregg Adams, National Cherry Blossom Festival®

65 left: © The Art Institute of Washington

65 right: ©National Cherry Blossom Festival®

66 & 67: ©Ron Engle, National Cherry Blossom Festival®

68: ©Keith Lukaszewski, National Cherry Blossom Festival®

69 left: ©National Cherry Blossom Festival®

69 right: ©Ron Engle, National Cherry Blossom Festival®

70 upper: Detail, *Children at Play*, Screen, 17th century, ink, color and gold on paper, 40.9 x 200.0 cm overall, Freer Gallery of Art, Smithsonian Institution, Washington, D.C.: Purchase

70 lower: Shunsho, Edo period (1603-1868), Inro, Lacquer, design of gold, silver and colors. Toledo Museum of Art: Gift of H.A. Fee, 1952.43

71: © Ron Engle, National Cherry Blossom Festival®

72 left: ©Simon Williams, National Cherry Blossom Festival®

72 right: © National Cherry Blossom Festival®

73 left: © F. T. Eyre, National Building Museum

73 right: ©Jennifer Swanson, National Cherry Blossom Festival®

74 upper: ©Ron Engle, National Cherry Blossom Festival®

74 lower: *Decorated Fans*, Edo period (1615-1868), Screen, Color, ink and gold on paper, 148 x 336 cm. Freer Gallery of Art, Smithsonian Institution, Washington, D.C.: Gift of Charles Lang Freer, F1897.94

75 left: Judy Rolfe, fan courtesy author

75 right: ©Wayne Fisher, National Cherry Blossom Festival®

76: Tsukioka Kogyo (1869-1927), *Pictures of Noh Play: Arashiyama*, 1902, Woodblock print, 228.6 x 331.79 mm. Scripps College, Claremont, California: 93.3.153

77 left: Freer Gallery of Art, Smithsonian Institution, Washington, D.C.

77 right: ©Ron Engle, National Cherry Blossom Festival®

78 left: ©Eric Long, National Cherry Blossom Festival®

78 upper right: ©Don Carter, National Cherry Blossom Festival®

78 lower right: ©Jerry Arnold, National Cherry Blossom Festival®

79: ©John Skowronski/Folio, Inc.

80-1: ©Marvin Ickow

82: ©John Swank

83: ©National Cherry Blossom Festival®

84 left: ©Marvin Ickow

85 right: ©Meher McArthur

86 left: ©John Swank

85 right: Margaret Pooler, National Arboretum

86 left: ©Keith Warren, J. Frank Schmidt & Son Co.

86 right: Alan Whittemore, National Arboretum

87 left: ©Steve Alterman

87 right: ©Nancy Buley, J. Frank Schmidt & Son Co.

88: A.R., National Park Service

89 left: ©Nancy Buley, J. Frank Schmidt & Son Co.

89 right: KANZAN, *Prunus lannesiana* 'Sekiyama' ©Mieko Ishikawa

90 left: Don Egolf, National Arboretum

90 right: Terry J. Adams, National Park Service

91: © Keith Warren, J. Frank Schmidt & Son Co.

92: ©Meher McArthur

93: ©Japan National Tourist Organization

94: ©Marvin Ickow

95 upper: National Park Service

95 lower: © Claire Carlin, National Cherry Blossom Festival®

97: ©Judy Rolfe

104: ©Japan National Tourist Organization

Bibliography

Anesaki, Masaharu. *Art, Life, and Nature in Japan* (Boston: Marshall Jones Company, 1933)

Ball, Jeff, "The Exquisite Ornamental Cherry," *American Forests*, March 22, 2001

Bauer, Helen and Carlquist, Sherwin. *Japanese Festivals* (Garden City, New York: Doubleday & Company, Inc., 1965)

Browning, Michael, "Like a Geisha," *The Palm Beach Post*, March 22, 1999

Buckland, Rosina. *Golden Fantasies: Japanese Screens from New York Collections* (New York: Asia Society, 2004)

Chamberlain, Basil Hall. *Things Japanese* (London and New York: Kegan Paul, Trench, Trubner & Co., Ltd., 1927)

Conder, Josiah. *The Flowers of Japan and the Art of Floral Arrangement* (Tokyo, New York, London: Kodansha International Ltd., 2004)

Dalby, Liza Crihfield. *Geisha* (Berkeley, Los Angeles, London: University of California Press, 1983)

Davis, F. Hadland. *Myths & Legends of Japan* (London: George G. Harrap & Company, 1912)

Fairchild, David. *The World Was My Garden, Travels of a Plant Explorer* (New York: Charles Scribner's Sons, 1938)

Gonick, Gloria Granz. Matsuri, *Japanese Festival Arts* (Los Angeles: UCLA Fowler Museum of Cultural History, 2002)

Hearn, Lafcadio. *Glimpses of Unfamiliar Japan* (Rutland, Vermont & Tokyo, Japan: Charles E. Tuttle Company, 1976)

Henderson, Harold G. *An Introduction to Haiku* (Garden City, New York: Doubleday & Company, 1958)

Hosley, William. *The Japan Idea, Art and Life in Victorian America* (Hartford, Connecticut: Wadsworth Atheneum, 1990)

Imperatore, Cheryl and MacLardy, Paul. *Kimono, Vanishing Tradition, Japanese Textiles of the 20th Century* (Atglen, Pennsylvania: Schiffer Publishing Ltd., 2001)

Jefferson, Roland M., "The History of the Cherry Blossom Trees in Potomac Park," *Introducing Modern Japan*, 1995

---------- and Fusonie, Alan E. *The Japanese Flowering Cherry Trees of Washington, D.C., A Living Symbol of Friendship* (Washington, D.C.: Agricultural Research Service, U.S. Department of Agriculture, National Arboretum, Contribution No. 4, 1977)

Joly, Henri L. *Legend in Japanese Art* (New York: John Lane Company, 1908)

Jonas, Patricia, Guest Editor. *Japanese-Inspired Gardens* (Brooklyn, New York: Brooklyn Botanic Garden, 2001)

The Junior League of Washington, Thomas Froncek, Editor. *An Illustrated History of The City of Washington* (New York: Alfred A. Knopf, 1977)

Kinoshita, June, and Palevsky, Nicholas. *Gateway to Japan* (Tokyo and New York: Kodansha International Ltd., 1990)

Kiritani, Elizabeth. *Vanishing Japan: Traditions, Crafts & Culture* (Vermont, Tokyo: Tuttle Publishing, 1995)

Kobayashi, Tadashi. *Ukiyo-E* (Tokyo, New York and San Francisco: Kodansha International Ltd., 1982)

Kodansha Encyclopedia of Japan (Tokyo and New York: Kodansha International Ltd., 1983)

Krasno, Rena. *Floating Lanterns and Golden Shrines; Celebrating Japanese Festivals* (Berkeley, California: Pacific View Press, 2000)

Kuitert, Wybe. *Japanese Flowering Cherries* (Portland, Oregon: Timber Press, 1999)

Manthorpe, Victoria, Editor. *Travels in the Land of the Gods (1898 – 1907), The Japan Diaries of Richard Gordon Smith* (New York: Prentice Hall Press, 1986)

Mitford, A.B. *Tales of Old Japan* (London and New York: Macmillan and Co., 1891)

Murase, Miyeko. *Bridge of Dreams, The Mary Griggs Burke Collection of Japanese Art* (New York: The Metropolitan Museum of Art, distributed by Harry N. Abrams, Inc., 2000)

O'Neill, Tom, "The Samurai Way," *National Geographic*, December 2003

Pauly, Philip J., "The Beauty and Menace of the Japanese Cherry Trees, Conflicting Visions of American Ecological Independence," Isis, 1996

Puette, William J. *The Tale of Genji by Murasaki Shikibu, A Reader's Guide* (Rutland, Vermont & Tokyo, Japan: Charles E. Tuttle Company, 1983)

Rexroth, Kenneth. *One Hundred Poems from the Japanese* (New York: New Directions, 1964)

Russell, Paul, "Americanizing the Japanese Cherry," *American Forests*, February 1926

--------- . *The Oriental Flowering Cherries* (Washington, D.C.: U.S. Department of Agriculture, Circular No. 313, March 1934)

Sakade, Florence. *Japanese Children's Favorite Stories* (Vermont, Tokyo: Tuttle Publishing, 2003)

Sakai, Atsuharu. *Japan in a Nutshell* (Yokohama: Yamagatsu Printing Company, 1949)

Scidmore, Eliza Ruhamah, "The Cherry-Blossoms of Japan, Their Season a Period of Festivity and Poetry," *The Century Magazine*, Vol.79, March 1910

----------, "Capital's Cherry Blossoms Gift of Japanese Chemist," *Washington Evening Star*, April 11, 1926

--------, "Cherry Trees are Blooming in Potomac Park," *The Sunday Star*, March 27, 1921

----------, *Jinrikisha Days in Japan* (New York: Harper & Brothers, 1891)

Shimizu, *Yoshiaki. Japan, the Shaping of Daimyo Culture, 1185-1868* (Washington, D.C.: National Gallery of Art, 1988)

Sites, Maud Kay. *The Japanese Cherry Trees in Washington, D.C.* (Baltimore, Maryland: Norman T.A. Munder, 1935)

Smith, Bradley. *Japan, A History in Art* (Tokyo: Toppan Printing Co., Ltd., 1964)

Unknown author. *Reference Guide* (Boring, Oregon: J. Frank Schmidt & Son Company, 2002)

Unknown author, "Reports of the Chronicler," *Records of The Columbia Historical Society*, Washington, D.C., 1930-1952

Uspensky, Mikhail. *One Hundred Views of Edo, Woodblock Prints by Ando Hiroshige* (Bournemouth, England: Parkstone, 1997)

Varley, Paul. *Japanese Culture, A Short History* (Rutland, Vermont: Charles E. Tuttle, 1973)

Vilhar, Gorazd, and Anderson, Charlotte. *Matsuri: World of Japanese Festivals* (Tokyo, Japan: Shufunotomo Co., Ltd., 1994)

Watson, William, Editor. *The Great Japan Exhibition, Art of the Edo Period 1600 – 1868* (London: Royal Academy of Arts in association with Weidenfeld and Nicolson, 1981)

Wichmann, Siegfried. *Japonisme, The Japanese Influence on Western Art in the 19th and 20th Centuries* (New York: Harmony Books, 1981)

Yoshikawa, Masso, "Romance of Japanese Cherry Blossoms Closely Related to Philosophy of Life," *Washington Sunday Star*, April 18, 1926

Websites Consulted

About.Com, www.japanese.about.com

Athenic Systems, www.treeguide.com

The Fan Circle International, www.fancircleinternational.org

Ikebana International, www.ikebanahq.org

Immortal Geisha, www.immortalgeisha.com

International Society of Arboriculture, www.treesaregood.com

Japan Forum, www.tjf.or.jp/eng/indexe/indexe.htm

Japan National Tourist Organization, www.jnto.jo.jp and www.japanwelcomesyou.com

Japan Travel and Living Guide, www.japan-guide.com

Judo Information, www.judoinfo.com

National Arbor Day, www.arborday.org

National Arboretum, www.usna.gov

National Cherry Blossom Festival, www.nationalcherryblossomfestival.org

National Conference of State Societies, www.statesocieties.org/cherry

National First Ladies Library, www.firstladies.org

National Park Service, www.nps.gov/nacc/cherry

Shimamura Music, www.shimamura.co.jp/english

The White House, www.whitehouse.gov/history/firstladies

Women in History, Lakewood Public Library, Ohio, www.lkwdpl.org